The
FOCALGUIDE
to
Bird
Photography

C000140182

THE ⓕ FOCALGUIDES TO

The
FOCALGUIDE
to
Bird
Photography

Michael W. Richards

Focal Press · London

Focal/Hastings House · New York

🔲🔲 British Library Cataloguing in Publication Data

Richards, Michael W
   The focalguide to bird photography.
   1. Photography of birds
   I. Title
   778.9'32   TR729.B5   79–41441

ISBN (excl. USA) 0 240 51048 8
ISBN (USA only) 0 8038 2384 3

All photographs are by the author, with thanks to the Royal Society for the Protection of Birds for use of copyright material.

Filmset and Printed in Great Britain by
Thomson Litho Ltd, East Kilbride, Scotland.

Contents

Birds in the Garden

Anyone interested in birds is able to see some of them from the comfort of a chair and, with ingenuity and patience, to photograph them too though possibly not from the chair. Wherever you live there are always some birds perching nearby. A garden, however small, undoubtedly attracts at least a few birds. Its potential is an exciting prospect even in these days of expanding suburbia for, paradoxically, this relatively new habitat is one that certain species have adapted to very well; it is all that is left from their original countryside homes.

Locations

Gardens are found in many different locations and with these differences go variations in the species and number of birds. Living in a wooded area you see a greater variety of birds visiting your garden than you would in a more open habitat like moorland or heath. Wherever you live a few migratory birds may pass through your vegetable patch during spring and autumn, though they are unlikely to stay more than one or two days.

For those new to bird photography the actual location of the garden is unimportant as it is always possible to see *something* even if it is only a pigeon or a cat. Cats are a nuisance when they appear just as you are about to take a photograph with the conditions just right, as of course, all the birds take flight. So before you start make sure all your feline friends are safely occupied elsewhere.

The first problem is to select a subject to photograph. Although almost everything that comes along is interesting it is just as well to have some idea of what you would like to end up with. Usually that is far from what you originally hoped for, but at least you have something to work towards. Unless there are some natural food plants in the garden your chances of photographing birds on predictable occasions are not very good as they have no reason to stay. Try to encourage them to remain in the garden for longer periods so that they become accustomed to the house and its surroundings. There are two ways of achieving this, both ways are beneficial to birds themselves. The first is to encourage them to feed by providing food and water, and the second is to prepare suitable nesting sites for them.

Bird tables

Feeding birds is a rewarding process when they seem to come from nowhere on those short cold winter days when the garden appears to be deserted. All food put outside attracts attention, and foxes, dogs, cats, rats and mice as well as birds will try to get any that is left on the ground. Therefore the best plan is to keep all food on a bird table. The basic requirements are simply a flat-topped surface on a post about 3 or 4 ft from the ground. There are also more elaborate designs with roofs to keep rain off the food. Have a top with a ridge round the edge to prevent food falling on the ground or being blown off by the wind. It also gives birds something to use as a perch which makes them less nervous.

The height of the table is a small point but one easily overlooked. Be sure that you can get the camera to a comfortable height relative to the table for photographing. It should be placed in a convenient part of the garden, perhaps near your kitchen or living-room window. Anywhere quiet near the house is likely to be attractive to many different species. By positioning your table a little further away near some suitable cover you will draw a greater variety of visitors. Some birds like to have a nearby refuge to fly to if danger threatens.

At the beginning the location of your table is not important as it takes birds several days to get used to any new object which suddenly appears. To start with they are always suspicious and keep well away. However it only takes a day or two for them to realize that there is food to be had, and gradually they come to use new feeding places regularly. A constant supply of food ensures that a good number of birds come down, and as these are seen by others to be feeding, more will in turn be attracted. It is interesting to keep your bird table well supplied throughout the winter as a considerable increase in the number of birds alighting there can be seen by the end of the season. Because they come to rely on your food supply, and may be coming some distance to get it, it is important to keep up regular feeds.

Food for the bird table

Wild bird seed obtainable from most pet shops, is the best food for your table. It can be supplemented with bread soaked in cooking oil or melted margarine; this is better for birds than dry bread. Suet and peanuts are popular, especially with the tit family. Nuts should be put into a wire feeder where they can be pecked without being carried off by birds, which would lessen your chances of getting pictures. These containers are also good protection against marauding squirrels.

Coconuts are popular with many birds, especially the tit family (see colour Section). They can be wedged firmly into a bush for stability, though watch out for cats that may be hiding there.

Bacon rind and carcasses of household meat with fat still left on them, can be tied to the bird table or hung from nearby branches. Push some bits of cheese into holes drilled into a post or tree stump; this makes it hard for birds to extract. Monkey nuts can be threaded with a needle and hung up, as can coconuts by sawing them in halves. A variety of food increases the opportunities for photographs. Unfortunately hanging food is always mobile but this can be overcome.

Take some time to read about birds' particular eating habits. You can learn a great deal this way because it applies not only to garden birds, but to all species. Talk to other people about their observations and experiences, and then try to illustrate a specific point as well as obtaining a bird portrait.

Points to consider

When birds start coming habitually to your table you can think about the ideal place to put it for photography. Several important

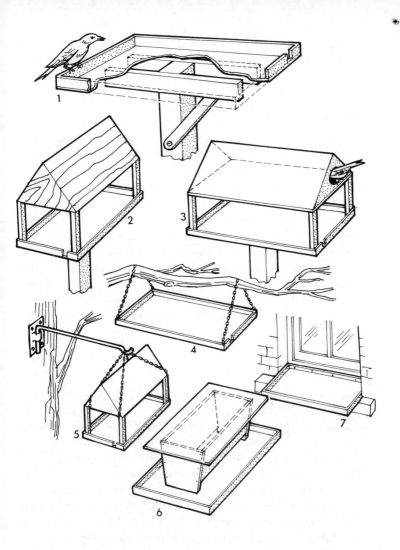

Figs 1–6 show examples of bird tables and feeding trays: **1** Flat topped
bird table. **2** Roofed bird table. **3** Roofed bird table incorporating a
nest box. **4** Open table top suspended from a tree. **5** Roofed table that
can be suspended from wall or tree. **6** Seed hopper with removable lid.
This remains on the ground. Mainly useful for ground seed eaters, of which
game birds are a good example. It can also be put on a post like a
conventional table. **7** Window box type of bird table.

factors must be considered first—the light source; the background; the surroundings; where to conceal yourself and the camera site or hide.

The light source

As photography at a bird table usually has to be done during winter when the days are shortest and the sun weak, it is essential to place the table where the midday sun falls squarely on it, i.e. behind the camera. In the Northern Hemisphere during December and January the days are at their shortest, so photography is restricted to between 10.00 am and 2.30 pm when the sun is at its brightest. This does not give the photographer much time. The sun is further away in winter and hangs lower in the sky, consequently giving a much 'warmer' or reddish-yellow light. It is therefore at its strongest and least warm in colour around midday. A blue filter can be attached to the lens to correct the yellow cast produced by the sun, thereby enabling you to obtain satisfactory results at any time of day.

The background

The second factor is the background. It is essential in bird photography to make this as clear and uncluttered as possible so that all the emphasis falls on the bird itself. This applies whether you use the house, the lawn or a hedge or shrub. The image of the bird will be 'lost' against a setting full of distracting details. A house, for example, can be made recognizable but well out of focus in the background, so that a picture can be obtained of a bird in a typical garden setting. Try to get the subject as far away from the background as possible. The cleanest background of all is an artificial one; a painted card, wood or even an old sheet.

The surroundings

Next, consider the surroundings. Trees and shrubs are important because they act as perches. Birds like to have somewhere to 'line-up' before coming down to feed, and to escape quickly should

14

anything startle them. Also they often take food away from the table to eat on a convenient perch, so if the table is some way off from such perches they must fly over longer distances and will be deterred from lingering in the immediate vicinity. This will give you fewer photographic opportunities. If there are no suitable shrubs nearby most birds will just as easily use a fence or washing line to rest on, but be sure there is something available for them when you put up your table. If nothing seems suitable you can always introduce your own perch; this has the advantage of being moveable so you can get the correct image in your camera.

Concealment

Having selected a good landing place for the birds the next consideration is the best position for yourself and your camera. A garden shed or a window in the house near enough for photography would make excellent ready-made hides. Open the shed window and cover it with some sacking in which you have made a hole for the lens and a slit for an 'eyepiece'. This must be stretched very tautly over the outside of the window frame and fixed with tacks so that it does not flap in the wind. The same can be done over the door. Do not photograph through glass unless you have to, although obviously it is not a popular move to open the living-room window on a freezing winter's day. The enthusiast might even remove a small piece of glass, but for most practical purposes a thorough wipe-over of the glass inside and out will give acceptable results. You must, however, check visually that it is free from warping and malformation which often occur with glass. Working from within the house, curtains can be used as a hide for yourself and the camera.

However, you may prefer to use the other end of the garden away from such cover. In this case make a hide that will be big enough for you and the camera, and sufficiently sturdy to be left out in all weathers. This ensures that birds become accustomed to it being there and even use it as a perch. They often try to land on my lens and occasionally bluetits find their way into the hide—but not to stay!

Do not introduce your hide on the projected day of photography.

The intrusion of a new object makes birds more hesitant and nervous.

Selecting camera and hide positions

Introduce your hide at some considerable distance from the table and, initially, use it simply to observe favourite perching places. This is to help you to set up your camera on the tripod in a position that gives you more than one possibility for photographs. If necessary move the hide over the camera. There is nothing worse than starting to photograph from a hide and realizing suddenly that it is in the wrong place and has to be moved.

Perches and plants

It is easy to introduce perches for birds to settle on round the bird table, and you may even be fortunate enough to have a tree leaning over it. If not, find a piece of dead wood that will stand up in the ground on a level with the table, and so be in the same plane of focus. So, by simply panning the camera on the tripod you have a variety of photographic possibilities for one set up. Make sure however that the backgrounds are always acceptable.

The longer you sit in the hide the more likelihood there is of noticing different shots, and after a while you can put up more perches to obtain birds in many situations. Having used one location for some time it is a good idea to move to a fresh part of the garden. If too many birds gather in one area the ground and perches become soiled with droppings after a time, and in some cases this can spread disease.

Certain birds such as sparrows, are very nervous and may take quite a few days to become accustomed to new perches or a repositioned bird table. The tit family, on the other hand, are much more adaptable and less shy. It is noticeable too, that some birds will not come down to feed unless others are already there, showing that there is no danger. A robin prefers to feed on his own and often arrives at the food first, his presence encouraging the rest to follow.

Observation tells you a lot about wild creatures so try setting up

1 Position the table where the midday sun falls squarely onto your subject. **2-3** Selection of the correct aperture for the effect you wish to obtain; **2** is a small *f* stop like *f*22; **3** is a wide *f* stop like *f*8. **4** A garden shed as a hide, using the door or the window.

your hide and camera by a favourite spot where a group of birds could be taken, preening their feathers or eating. You can obtain a wealth of information which would otherwise go unnoticed and many photographic opportunities would be wasted. Make your perches the right size for the type of bird you expect. A large branch for a small bird to alight on can make it seem even smaller.

Setting the scene

Birds tend to favour certain sorts of shrubs and trees especially in cold weather, berry-bearing shrubs being a typical example. Therefore try to get pictures of birds attacking these bushes. In the long term it pays off to plant suitable native shrubs to encourage birds into your garden. It will take some time for these to become large enough to support food so it may not be of immediate benefit to you photographically. It is, of course, only necessary to have a few leaves or one branch in a photograph if it incorporates a close up of a bird. Young plants can be placed against interesting backdrops for this. Cuttings of holly, for example, can be arranged behind a suitable perch, either by putting the stalks into the soil or into bottles of water which will help to stop them wilting. Be careful when choosing these plants to get the correct type for the photograph; a sparrow against a foreign cactus does not look authentic. Do not pick out dark evergreens like yew (*Taxus baccata*) as they make a very sombre backcloth unless there is a lot of light falling on them.

Because there is no holly (*Ilex acquifolium*) in my neighbourhood, I once arranged some branches as a setting for a robin in the snow. Soon a blackbird arrived and, there being no other food, soon stripped the holly of all its berries, completely destroying my careful set up. This episode took me by surprise and emphasized two noteworthy points: (1) I did not get a picture of the blackbird eating the berries, as perhaps I should have, because the berries were too far back for the amount of extension I had on the lens and I was not able to focus back to where the holly was. So when the larger blackbird arrived even had I been able to alter the focus without moving the camera, it would still have been too big in the frame as I was too close to it. You may be fortunate enough to

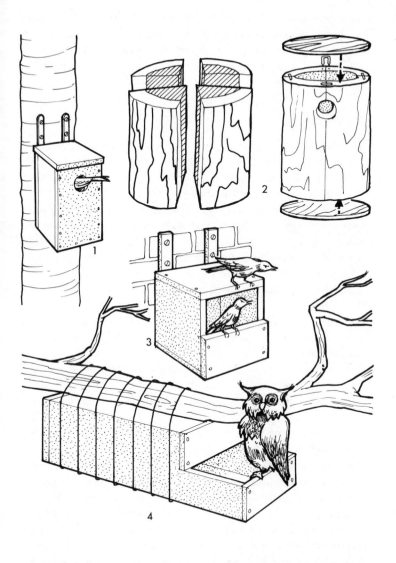

Bird nesting boxes. **1** Enclosed nest box for smaller birds with removable lid for inspection and cleaning out in the winter. **2** Simple enclosed box made from a log of wood. **3** Open-fronted nest box. This will attract different kinds of birds. **4** Owl nesting box positioned high up in a tree.

have two cameras, one with a shorter focal length lens focused to cover this kind of unexpected event. (2) It is worth mentioning that the birds might have eaten all the berries before I got any photographs at all, so keep some fresh berries back just in case.

Nesting Boxes

The mechanised agriculture of today has destroyed much of the traditional breeding cover for birds by creating bigger fields for greater production. There is, therefore, a shortage of suitable nesting habitat and species disappear from these areas.

Nesting boxes can be put up in your garden in various places to encourage winter feeders and others to breed where you can see and enjoy them. Birds will be grateful for this provision as they make perfect sites for a number of them. For some time I have had a nesting box on the side of the house by a window and it is used every year. It is ideal for taking photographs from indoors.

It is better for the occupants if the box does not face south as it will be baked by the sun. Place it where it is in shadow for some of the day. Birds are usually territorial in their breeding habits so do not put the boxes too near to each other.

They can be of many types. Some are enclosed, the size of the opening determining the size of bird which is likely to nest there. Open nest boxes attract flycatchers and robins. All these are simple to fix to the side of the house, posts in the ground or on trees. The higher they are the better to be out of the reach of cats, but do not place them too high for photographing.

It is possible to make a nest box from the top of your bird table so that your opportunities for taking pictures need not alter with the change of season; only perhaps in the number of species. The best time to introduce boxes is during winter when there are many birds in the garden who will investigate anything new. If you have a nest box incorporated into your table you must stop putting out food in early spring. Any bird deciding to use the box will constantly defend it as its own territory, from others. This might result in a complete failure to breed if too many birds are in the area.

Tits have been seen entering boxes in December and January,

prospecting for their first springtime nest. A winter introduction will help birds to find the boxes more easily. If you put them up too late in the season the birds may not get used to them until the following year.

Be sure to have boxes with removable lids so that they can be emptied and cleaned out after the birds have left. This helps to prevent disease and too much nesting material piling up.

Nest boxes are photographed in a similar way to that described for bird tables, unless you use electronic flash, which is dealt with in chapter 5.

You may want to progress to something more adventurous than a nesting box, such as natural nest sites. Summer's warmer weather produces different activities in birds; more nests hatch out which necessitates the adults hunting for large quantities of food which is now abundant. You should get some excellent shots of birds in their normal surroundings, provided you have enough patience to go slowly so as not to cause them to desert the nests.

Equipment and Film for Bird Photography

There is no need to spend large amounts of money on the equipment you need to take photographs of birds. Despite all the publicity for the latest electronic device or camera feature, you can do very well with quite unpretentious means. A camera is only a light-tight box and no matter what amount you spend, the cheapest camera in the right hands can produce better photographs than the most expensive one in the hands of someone who has very little idea of what he is doing.

Choosing your camera

From the choice of cameras available there are several important things to consider if you are to have sufficient versatility to tackle all the aspects of bird photography. Not every feature that a camera offers is vital; some extras can be very expensive yet of limited value in this particular branch of photography.

The first consideration in choosing a camera is the format of film that it takes. A camera that uses 35 mm film is the most versatile and lightweight type and the quality of picture obtainable is adequate for most purposes. Economically it also compares favourably with larger formats. Large cameras can, however, be used to advantage in certain situations and, for their gain in picture area and quality, together with certain mechanical advantages, are valued by professional photographers. But they do have technical and physical differences which make them harder to use successfully, and they can be very expensive.

In this book it is assumed that the reader is working with 35 mm equipment, although in most cases the techniques described apply equally to the larger format camera.

Single lens reflex (SLR)

This is the basic camera type for all bird photography. Its advantages include the reflex viewing whereby you can see through the actual taking lens which shows you exactly what image area you are going to capture on film. This is very important: it should ensure that you do not cut off the bird's tail or feet.

Features of the single lens reflex that are particularly important for bird photography are as follows:

Bright reflex viewing with clear focusing; a range of shutter speeds up to 1/1000 second; scope for interchanging lenses to obtain different sized images of the subject (i.e. different angles of view); synchronization for flash; through-the-lens (TTL) metering.

The reflex viewing may be better for you with one camera than another, particularly if you wear spectacles. Look through several cameras and select the one that is most comfortable for you to see the image and any readouts or figures also visible in the viewfinder.

Almost all SLRs offer a full range of shutter speeds though a few models omit the lower ones (e.g. below 1/15 second). A model that has a top speed of 1/1000 second can, in certain aspects of bird photography, score over one limited to 1/500 second (assuming that the shutter is accurate enough to actually give those speeds, which a poor quality or old one may not). Synchronization for flash is to be found on virtually all SLR cameras and the only question here is the shutter speed available for use with electronic flash units.

Through-the-lens (TTL) metering, now very common in cameras, is useful because it measures the light level from the actual image area seen by the lens. With this facility being built into the camera there is no need to carry a separate light meter around. The less you have to carry the better. However, there are drawbacks. In some circumstances a TTL meter may give you a false reading, so it is necessary to use it with intelligence rather than follow its exposure determination blindly.

Choosing a camera is ultimately a matter of personal preference and economics. Within your price range there are likely to be several different makes available. Look at as many of these as you can and see which one seems to handle best. It must feel 'right' in your hands and be easy to see through because you should always be relaxed when releasing the shutter. Decide on the necessary features and remember particularly that bayonet-fitting lenses can be changed more quickly than the older screw types.

Provided your camera has all the features mentioned above (except perhaps TTL metering) it can be applied to almost any kind of job. Even if it has no built-in exposure meter and you have to take all readings of the light level with a separate hand meter, the results obtained will be the same.

The most expensive cameras do probably have a longer and more trouble-free working life than those costing less, and they are built for professionals who put far more films through them than would any amateur, so these advantages are not important to you.

Non-reflex cameras

With non-reflex cameras the photographer views the subject through a separate viewfinder which may not give exactly the same view as the lens that takes the picture, either because it is in a different position or because the image from the taking lens is of a different size. Although you can learn from experience what results to expect it is never very satisfactory to use this type of camera in the field as you tend to forget to compensate for the slightly different framing (due to the effects of parallax differences between the lens and the viewfinder). For birds you are nearly always working at close range and therefore it is important to know that you have the whole bird exactly in the frame.

Aperture and shutter speed

If you have never used a camera before it is most important to know how it works and what results to expect. All cameras control exposure by variable shutter speeds and lens apertures. The combination of the use of these two controls is vital to the end result. These must be used not merely to control the amount of light reaching the film, but for their other properties—according to the shooting conditions and the particular lens demanded by them.

24

Robin *(Erithacus rubecula)* Nesting in a garden shed.
Electronic flash was essential as it was very dark outside.

Above   Puffin   *(Fratercula arctica)*
Carefully approached without a hide.

Opposite   Gannet *(Sula bassana)*
Carefully approached in a colony without a hide; 180 mm lens.

Above Barnacle Geese *(Branta leucopsis)*
Taken in the open hand-holding a 400 mm lens. A free flying flock in a wildfowl collection.

Opposite, top Wheatear *(Oenanthe oenanthe)*
Taken from a car with a long focal length lens (1000 mm). A migrating bird remaining for a few days.

Opposite, bottom Arctic tern *(Sterna paradisea)*
Alighting at its nest. Photographed without a hide.

Water rail *(Rallus aquaticus)*
Taken in sub-zero temperatures which can be very uncomfortable but well worth it.
Flash has been used with a larger format camera.

Reed warbler *(Acrocephalus scirpaceus)*
On a perch near its nest.

Blue tit *(Parus caeruleus)*
Carefully controlled by making the coconut stable and using flash.

Exposure control

The aperture diaphragm in a camera lens can be likened to the iris of the eye; if you open it up it lets more light through the lens and into the camera, and if you close it the amount of light passing through is reduced.

The different sizes of the aperture are calibrated in regular steps and are called *f* stops. Each time you decrease the *f* stop (e.g. from *f*8 to *f*11) you are halving the amount of light passing through the lens. The shutter speeds are arranged in equivalent steps. So each increase of shutter speed (e.g. from 1/30—1/60 second) halves the *time* for which that amount of light is allowed to pass compared with the previous one. Adjustment of aperture or speed in the opposite direction doubles the quantity of light or the time for which it passes. For any given exposure if you increase one and decrease the other by the same amount there is no change to the overall exposure. This can easily be seen by looking at the speed and aperture calibrations set against one another on a light meter.

Manual and auto exposure

The eye automatically lets in the right amount of light to obtain a good image of the object in view. Cameras are not quite so efficient, though some of the more advanced ones do offer a very high level of automation.

In each case the brightness of the scene is assessed by the TTL meter and this can be translated into an exposure setting. For many cameras, to set the correct exposure, the diaphragm or shutter setting ring must be adjusted to align an indicator to a fixed or a moving index (e.g. follow pointer) as determined by the exposure meter. On a fully automatic camera this function is taken care of by the camera itself.

On some automatic cameras once you have set the shutter speed you need, the built-in TTL exposure meter automatically sets the aperture diaphragm to the appropriate *f* stop for the scene. This is known as *shutter priority* auto exposure control. On others, you set the aperture you want and the camera sets the corresponding shutter speed according to the brightness of the scene. This is called *aperture priority* metering control. Certain cameras offer a choice of these modes of operation. In the majority of cases the camera also allows you to set the shutter speed and aperture manually without reference to the built-in metering device (manual override).

In practice there may be little difference between the operation of an aperture or shutter priority camera if, by adjustment of one, the other automatically compensates, and both the aperture and shutter speed may be read off a scale that is continuously visible. Cameras with fully automatic exposure control are generally more expensive than those requiring some degree of manual adjustment.

Hand meters

The advantage of a hand held exposure meter is that it can be used to make selective exposure readings from various parts of the scene without moving the camera which may be set up on a tripod or other rigid support.

A hand meter may be used like a meter built in to the camera, for measuring the light *reflected from* the subject. But many hand meters have a special diffuser which allows light readings to be made from light *incident* on the subject. Even simple meters often have this facility. Having previously set the film ASA speed, the meter tells you what shutter speed and aperture combination to set for the brightness of the scene. You then set these manually on the camera.

Incident readings

The meter is held in the subject position (or an equivalent place) and pointed towards the camera or in the equivalent direction (i.e. behind the camera) if used from the camera site. The reading thus obtained represents the light falling on to a subject consisting for the most part of mid-grey tones. You would have to compensate exposure for a particularly dark or light coloured bird, for greatest accuracy.

Reflected readings

With a hand held reflected light meter or one built in to the camera it is rarely possible to take a reading off a bird itself. So a reading has to be taken off a similar subject of a similar colour in the same sort of surroundings, which is usually accurate for most purposes. When shooting colour transparencies it is better to take a reading from a lighter part of the picture as you must not overexpose the highlight areas. In black and white it is important to take a reading from the shadow area as only by exposing for the shadows will enough light reach the emulsion to record detail there.

Always remember to use the same light meter so that you learn from your results how accurate it is and what special properties it has. It therefore does not matter what type of meter you have as your results will soon show how to produce accurate exposure from it. When getting to know the meter try to take a range of exposures to discover which is best for other occasions.

The shutter

Most 35 mm reflex cameras have shutters in the form of an opaque blind positioned immediately in front of the surface of the film. Within this blind is a variable slit whose width is controlled by the speed selected on the camera itself. Therefore when the blind travels across to expose the film, light is passed through only for as long as it takes the gap in the blind to move across. It is fairly easy to see that a larger gap will take longer than a small gap. The shutter speeds are marked on a control dial and these normally range from 1—1/1000 second or, in some cases from 4—1/200 second or 1/2—1/500 second. The usual sequence is as follows: 4, 2, 1, 2, 4, 8, 15, 30, 60, 125, 250, 500, 1000, 2000. The first four digits represent whole seconds and those that follow are fractions of a second at intervals equivalent to half the exposure time of the preceding digit. A slightly different sequence from that above appears on some old cameras.

There are two additional settings: on 'B' you can physically hold the shutter open for any length of time you like, either by keeping your finger on the button or cable release or by locking them in the depressed position. A locking cable release avoids direct manual contact with the camera during such time exposures and so ensures a steadier image. A few very old cameras have a 'T' (time) setting. By pressing the shutter the lens remains open indefinitely until it is pressed a second time. For 'B' and 'T' exposures it is essential to have the camera well supported e.g. on a firm tripod.

Film speed and choice of film

Whatever form of metering method you use, in every case the built-in or hand meter must be pre-set to take account of the sensitivity to light of the particular film that has been loaded. Films are labelled with an ASA or DIN (film speed) rating to tell you how sensitive to light they are. Thus, films of different speeds would require different settings for correct exposure under the same conditions. The camera or hand meter has a dial marked with ASA (or DIN) speeds and thus must be set to correspond with the figure marked on the film carton.

The film stock you decide to use is very important since there is a large selection to choose from both in specification and manufacturer. There are both black and white and colour films available and these come in films for making prints (colour or black and white) or slides (mostly colour). Black and white transparencies are seldom used today as colour is so popular. Black and white negatives, however, allow you more control over your results than colour.

All films are categorized by ASA (or DIN) speed and the differences must be understood. A high ASA rating means the film is fast (highly light-sensitive) and can therefore be used in worse light conditions than a film with a lower rating. High speed films are not used all the time because they also have disadvantages. Most obviously, the grain structure of the emulsion tends to be coarse. This is undesirable in natural history photography as the plumage of birds, for example, may not be so well defined. In colour, high speed films do not have very much exposure latitude (i.e. if you slightly overexpose or underexpose a shot, it will be very obviously incorrect). Slower films in colour tend to be more tolerant; even with slight errors you still have acceptable results.

Slow films also have a much finer grain structure giving very sharp results and give especially good black and white enlargements. In colour, slow speed films usually have better colour saturation giving a richness of colour sometimes absent from higher speed films. Some people hold particular makes of film as far better than others; others may say the reverse. The only way to choose is to try different makes for yourself and see which gives you the most satisfactory result. Colour quality is a very subjective matter; although transparency films may have a bias towards a particular colour, this is usually thought by its users to be a desirable feature.

For black and white, start with a medium speed (125 ASA) film which will give very good results on general subjects in average conditions. For colour use a 64 ASA film which, again, will give you good colour saturation and a fair amount of exposure latitude so that you can get accustomed to using the rest of your equipment, and also obtain acceptable results.

Depth of field

Stopping down the aperture diaphragm, in addition to letting in less light also increases the range of distances in the picture that appear sharply focused—a very useful feature. This so-called 'depth of field' is literally the amount of depth in the picture that is acceptably sharp when the finished print or transparency is looked at under certain more or less standard viewing conditions.

The available depth of field increases not only with a smaller aperture, but also the greater the distance the lens is focused upon and the shorter the focal length of the particular lens in use.

Using the depth of field scale

If you look at any lens barrel you will see on either side of the focusing scale index, pairs of lines marked with the normal aperture scale. (These indicate the limits of field depth at each aperture setting according to the focused distance—i.e. how far beyond and in front of the subject the scene will appear sharp when the lens is correctly focused on the subject.

Even when focused at close range the great field depth of a wide angle lens makes it possible to prefocus the lens and still manage to get most of the photograph sharp. The diagram shows a wide angle lens set to take a photograph at *f*16. Let us suppose that the requirement of this photograph is to have as much as possible of the subject sharp right up to infinity. It is possible to determine this without looking through the viewfinder, though you obviously have to compose a photograph as far as possible by using the finder. In the example the infinity marked on the lens is levelled with the *f*16 marked on the right of the centre focus. By reading the figure against the left hand *f*16 it can be seen that everything from 1.1 metres to infinity is going to be acceptably sharp if *f*16 is used. Focusing becomes relatively unimportant when using such a small aperture. Even *f*11 gives a good range and it should be very possible to use fairly fast shutter speeds in good light with a fast film stock. Shooting in conditions where movement allows little time for focusing, a prefocused lens can produce photographs you never thought you would get; it is well worth taking a lot as one or two always seem much better than all the rest.

Sometimes you may not want the far distance to be in focus and in this case you might prefer to work from the other side of the focus scale and set the aperture against the nearest point you want in sharp focus—say, the nearest members of a group of birds—and hope that you have enough depth to include those further off as well. It is much better to have the foreground subject sharp and the background unsharp than the other way round.

Lenses for bird photography

Having decided on your camera you have to choose the lenses to use with it. Popular opinion always seems to assume that to photograph birds you need a very long focal length lens, and once in possession of such a lens you cannot fail to obtain excellent results. Unfortunately, this is simply not the case, and many people have spent a lot of money on a lens with as long a focus as 600 mm or more, only to find that they just do not get the quality and picture size they want.

It is true that for distant subjects a long focus lens is unnecessary (and this is discussed later), but for work at close range, as with a

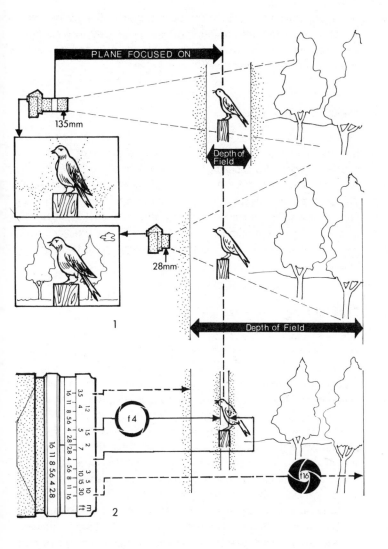

1 Showing the effect of using different lenses at the same aperture on the same subject: the image remaining the same size in each case, but the background being very different indeed. **2** Depth of field scale on a lens can tell you how much of the subject will be sharp by reading off the distances either side of the centre.

bird table, satisfactory results can be obtained with a 135 mm lens, which is ideal for bird photography. It enables you to work fairly near to the subject without being in its way and to get a reasonably sized image as well.

Close focusing: tubes

The best distance for working with small birds is about 5 ft. Because this may be the minimum focus distance of the lens it allows no scope for focusing should the bird move closer. So, in addition to the lens, you need extension tubes or rings or bellows. The principle of these is to position the lens further forward than normal and so focus closer than you otherwise could. Tubes can be used singly, or in combination for shooting very small subjects. Bellows do the same job but allow continous adjustment of the lens extension.

Determining image size

The best way to find out how much extension to put on your lens is to decide on what size bird you hope to photograph as, clearly, you need to be much closer to a member of the tit family than to a pigeon, and therefore will need more extension for the former.

For example, to obtain the right size for a small bird select a similar sized object like an apple, while still indoors, and choose a tube to see the image this gives you. To fill the frame with this you will probably find that two tubes are necessary. With this established it will give you a very good idea of the distance to work at to get a similar sized image of a small bird in your viewfinder.

With extension tubes it is possible to go from a fairly distant close up to perhaps just the head and shoulders of a bird. Extension of the lens in this way does, however, mean you also have to increase the exposure. This is best done from experience or can be worked out from the formula:

$$\text{Exposure Required} = \frac{\text{Exposure from}}{\text{Light Meter}} \times \frac{(\text{Total Extension})^2}{(\text{Focal Length of lens})^2}$$

Close up lenses

These are additional elements of different powers which screw onto the front of the lens like a filter, enabling a closer focus to be obtained. No light is lost as with other extensions, although too much glass in front of the lens can affect the quality of the result.

Bellows

These are more expensive but give extensions comparable to tubes yet may be adjusted for extension without the need to take the lens off each time. These are therefore considerably easier to use.

Neither tubes or bellows necessarily allow the operation of an automatic diaphragm. If not, the subject must be viewed through a lens which is stopped down to the working aperture which at small f stops may be quite dim. If this is unsatisfactory and you need to view your subject through a fully open operature then it is possible to use a double cable release and special auto ring which stops down the lens just before it fires the shutter.

Using extension tubes or bellows does permit adjustment of the image to any size/distance relationship likely to be required. Bellows are more convenient when working close to your subject as the bird may appear too close or too large in the frame, which calls for last-minute changes. Where the bird is too close it is worth turning the camera on its side to try and fit it into an upright format.

Macro lenses

These are lenses which have their own built in extension enabling them to focus much closer than the corresponding conventional lens and still retain infinity. They are very useful for bird photography, although expensive. The 135 mm is ideal for any situation where extension might otherwise have to be used.

Long focal length lenses

The type of lens you use may limit the shutter speed you can set to take the picture because there may only be enough light to use your lens at its widest aperture (wide open). As many long focal length lenses have a maximum aperture of only f8 or f5.6 using such lenses is not always something to recommend. It is always much better to stop down a lens if you possibly can as it will then perform better by giving sharper results with the additional depth of field. Only the more expensive lenses perform well at full aperture. Mirror lenses cannot be stopped down and so are committed to a fixed aperture but this need not necessarily be a disadvantage.

It certainly is not necessary to spend a fortune on a long focal length lens. Any lens leaving a factory is tested to perform within certain limits, and with cheaper lenses the margins of acceptability are wider, but it is still possible to end up with a very good lens for not very much money. The focal length of the lens also dictates the maximum aperture available.

With a few highly expensive and unwieldy exceptions, medium long focal length lenses have a larger maximum aperture than those of greater focal length. Therefore do not try to use a lens of longer focal length than necessary. They do not give quite the same image quality as medium long focal lengths; they compress perspective, and this gives a false impression of a bird's form.

Zoom lenses

Another way to obtain the correct size image in your viewfinder is to use a zoom lens which is of variable focal length. Zoom lenses include those designed to go from wide angle to telephoto, or from a short telephoto setting to a longer one.

They have the great advantage of being able to change focal length while still mounted on the camera which allows you to take pictures in unexpected circumstances, for example, if you are hoping for a small bird with a 200 mm setting and instead a large one appears, you simply change to, say, 100 mm.

Unfortunately these lenses are usually not of such good optical quality as an equivalent fixed focal length lens. They tend to give better image quality in the middle of the frame than at the edges, especially when used at the extremes of their focal length range and at maximum aperture.

Converters

Converters, or tele extenders, fit between the camera and lens and multiply the focal length of any lens by 2 to 3x, depending on the type. Being less expensive than an extra lens, they are an attractive proposition to many people.

As with zoom lenses the usefulness of converters depends on your needs. If you only want your pictures to project on to a screen they do not have to be as good technically as if you are shooting on negative or slide film from which you are going to make prints. For the latter purpose, converters are only going to partially satisfy you. They are useful to start with on garden birds as they can provide an inexpensive way to help you get used to different focal lengths of lens. When a converter is used with any lens there is always a loss in quality from that lens. Results disappoint because the tendency is to hold out great expectations from them. Another disadvantage is that they alter the aperture settings on the lens you are using them with by two or more stops. So, if your widest stop is normally f5.6 then with a 2x converter it will effectively be f11. This clearly makes it difficult when weather conditions are not good, and may rule out possible use.

Tripods

For bird photography a good solid tripod is essential. For all the inconvenience of its weight when walking long distances, to have a firm stand for the camera is worth all the rest of the trouble you have gone to.

Wooden tripods are hard to find but do make very firm bases, and do not reflect bright sunlight. Metal tripods have some drawbacks. Their bright finish can be conspicuous when being carried and can sometimes show through a gap in a hide. They often have blunt-ended feet which cannot be pushed into the ground, and the centre column can be a mixed blessing as it prevents the tripod going very low so that working from ground level becomes difficult. However some tripods have a mount at the base of the column so the camera can be fitted upside down and this enables a fairly low viewpoint to be achieved.

The metal can always be sprayed black or dark green which helps, though it tends to chip off again, and very soon your new tripod looks twenty years old!

It is essential to be able to pan in a horizontal plane so make sure the top of the tripod is level. Similarly, to be able to change to a vertical format is extremely useful.

Remote release

It is possible to fire the shutter of your camera from a distance by means of a very long cable release. These releases are available in several forms. The easiest to obtain and use is a long air release which works effectively over short ranges. An air release is simply a length (e.g. 8 metres) of hollow rubber tubing with a rubber air ball on one end and a plunger in the form of a cable release on the other. By pressing the rubber ball the air pressure pushes the plunger and releases the shutter. An air release can be made longer though the air pressure becomes reduced and this makes it harder to fire. I have heard of a bicycle pump being used in place of the rubber ball to give a greater force of air to the shutter release.

Another method is to use an electrical release which has the advantage of being as capable of use over a much greater distance, and it can be fired without much delay. An air release creates a slight pause between pressing the rubber ball and firing the shutter. Electrically the shutter release is made from a solenoid which throws the release pin into the camera as the button at the other end is pressed to complete the electrical circuit. This can be troublesome if the camera is not absolutely steady, as the whole of this movement can be very violent and cause camera shake during the exposure. It is also possible to fire the camera by radio which allows you to work over a large area without connecting cords or cables. However, licences are needed in the UK to operate this kind of apparatus and they are expensive. So it is worth familiarizing yourself with local laws before trying to buy the equipment.

Finally, it is possible to make a homemade cable release which can be fired by a piece of thread. This requires a mousetrap. Drill a hole in the base for a cable release. As the trap release it lets the metal arm fall onto the cable release, thereby firing the camera.

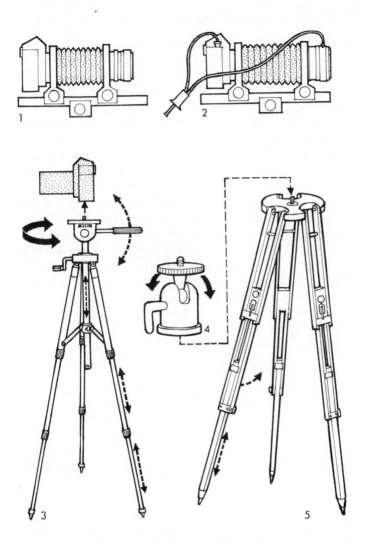

1 Bellows attached to camera and lens. 2 Double cable release to fire camera and stop lens down at the same time. (Automatic bellows do not require this). 3 Conventional metal tripod with pan and tilt head. 4 Ball and socket head which can be used instead of the pan and tilt head in 3 above. 5 A very basic design of a wooden tripod. These have no centre column and can therefore be made to go very low.

Application of remote control

Being able to fire the shutter of your camera from a distance has obvious appeal when working in the field. Clearly it is easier to be able to introduce your camera on a tripod to a situation, than a much larger hide, but this method of photographing birds both at bait and at the nest, has two serious disadvantages. You cannot always be sure exactly how much of your bird is going to be sharp as you are unable to compose the picture in any way once the camera is set up. You therefore have to have a very good idea of just where the bird will be. The other drawback is that usually camera transport must be advanced to the next frame after each exposure and this causes considerable disturbance and is not very satisfactory. If you own a motor drive or auto winder (which automatically winds the film on after each exposure) this can be overcome. Such accessories are, unfortunately, expensive and not something that every amateur can afford.

Having set up your camera in this kind of situation, it is essential that you hide yourself somewhere to observe and take pictures. Try to get into a position which is as nearly in line with the camera as possible; this will give most help in seeing what view the camera is getting, and consequently what sort of shot you end up taking.

Birds at Bait

The best way to begin at a particular site in order to lure as many different species as possible, is to provide various foods and, during the following few days, notice what birds are arriving. Different species have individual eating habits; some birds are fruit eaters, some prefer seeds and others like meat and fat. See which foods are preferred and select the kind that is attracting the bird you wish to photograph.

The right setting

Remember when taking your photograph, to get your subject in as natural a setting as possible. A woodpecker, for example, looks better on a branch than on the ground, although there is an exception: the European green woodpecker (*Picus viridis*) likes ants and can often be seen probing for them in the soil. The great spotted woodpecker (*Dendrocopus major*) eats fat and cheese and, if you have pushed lumps of these into holes drilled into a post or tree stump, will come down to peck at them. Other birds are likely to use this arrangement too, and you will soon have a lot of exciting activity going on. It often ends up with you obtaining photographs of a number of different species, except the one you originally hoped for!

Most small and medium sized birds are attracted to bird tables. The key to success is regular feeding. If started early enough during the fall months it may well be that migrants moving south will be encouraged to stay, sometimes throughout the winter if the food is sufficiently enticing.

Your garden is only the beginning; there are many other possibilities with birds never likely to come near cultivated ground. These occur in more remote and specialized habitats such as marshes, heaths, farmland and moors. Whatever the location it is the consistency of food supply that encourages birds to come regularly.

Regular feeding

This may limit your choice of location as travelling becomes a time-consuming activity. Food must be put out daily and, after a week or two, the birds will come to rely on it. With larger birds this usually takes longer. It is more difficult to keep up a regular supply of food for carrion eaters which like dead rabbits or other meat; this is very expensive even over a short period.

Grain is a useful food item in winter and frequent scattering of an area can result in a number of seed-eaters. Put grain out near water for a chance of waterfowl. Using food as a bait in this way has proved to be most successful in Britain where large flocks of waterfowl are constantly lured in front of public hides which provide excellent photographic opportunities. In this situation a 400 mm lens on 35 mm format is ideal.

Food left on the table in a single heap will soon be dispersed and scattered over the ground by the birds who will then, themselves, spread out more widely over a large area leaving you with nothing in front of your camera. So, to avoid this and to ensure that your food supplies remain fresh and cannot be removed all at once, have some wire containers for nuts and suet. Seeds (especially sunflower seeds), grain and other loose food can be placed in a hopper so that only the seeds at the bottom are available for eating and the remainder stay dry and fresh until the food below is eaten and it is released.

Selecting the right perch is important; it must look natural for the species using it. Change the perch when you have got the pictures of the bird you wanted, otherwise all your photographs will begin to look the same. See that the perch is not too flimsy as it will have a tendency to move a lot when a bird lands on it, and you will be unable to obtain a good picture. Also, the weight of the bird could make the branch or perch move out of the picture frame and possibly out of focus. This is especially frustrating when using remote control, as you cannot check framing and focus without approaching the camera.

1 An example of using remote control for action photography with birds near a bird table. An air release is used to fire the camera and computerized flash of the small bird.   **2** Low angle baiting to bring the birds down for a more dramatic angle. A particularly useful set up if using flash, as stands and flash heads need not be too obtrusive and tall. Choose a suitable background.

Photographing birds in bushes

In this situation the hide needs to be placed in a semi-concealed position slightly further away than from more controlled lures. Five metres (approx: 5 yards) is suitable, and a longer focal length lens will ensure that you obtain a good sized image. Anything between 300 mm and 500 mm is adequate for this distance and it should be possible to cover any one part of the bush from the hide.

Migrating birds rely on natural foods like berries, as much as resident birds, so you may have opportunities to try for species that do not stay in your garden for long. If there are many berry-bearing bushes in your neighbourhood birds are, unfortunately, not going to have the same pull to 'your' particular bush as you would like. Thrushes and blackbirds are fond of fallen apples which can be used as bait in winter with great success. Tying them to branches allows you to photograph birds sitting naturally in trees, as well as hopping about the ground.

To prevent birds from landing where you cannot focus on them, tie small bits of foliage and tufts of grass to the branches. By reducing the number of available landing places birds are more likely to alight in front of the camera.

Conceal your hide as well as possible as birds are suspicious of all new objects that appear. Set it up the day before you intend starting work, as the less time you spend in the vicinity of the prospective bush the better, and the birds will not be kept away too long. As soon as you enter the hide put the camera lens in position as quickly as possible so that all external movement soon stops, and make sure that you yourself are well hidden. Lenses of 300 mm–500 mm can be long in physical length; do not have too much protruding from the hide as any movement will be noticed by the wary bird which will probably fly off. Leave only 2 or 3 inches of the lens out of the hide keeping the rest of the camera inside. Move slowly and carefully so that you do not jerk the camera. A tripod is necessary for this. Hand holding a lens leads to failure since it is impossible to hold it absolutely still for any length of time. The birds will accept the lens only if it is completely still. Some movement will, of course, be necessary—panning the camera from side to side to bring the bird into frame, for example. 'Panning' is to move the camera in a horizontal plane about a fixed axis. If you have chosen your bush well the birds should start arriving within half an hour. Once they appear do not do anything at all. Let them become accustomed to the surroundings which include you and your hide. The longer you wait the more birds will fly down and the more confidence they will have in the location. A sudden movement or the noise of the camera too soon can frighten them away and they may not return again. Once they settle down and starting feeding you can start taking photographs.

Creating situations

A feeding sparrow (*Passer domesticus*) will soon attract others of the species and they are very interesting to watch. They are always incredibly alert. It is possible to watch as many as 50 of them feeding at the roadside on spilt corn; at the slightest noise they will all fly up into the air—which makes them hard to approach and very difficult to photograph.

Because large quantities of food do not necessarily occur naturally they have to be provided and often cause artificial situations such as concentrating the birds into one area. This may not be normal for those particular birds. However, there are photographic advantages, since birds thrown together in this way show aggression by fighting, and animosity by display to each other. These are interesting activities to capture on film.

During early visits to the food supply birds are likely to be nervous for they are always cautious in new surroundings, as well as wary of other birds. Some species become very belligerent towards others, but, after a few days a pattern emerges and then photography becomes easier.

Birds and water

Water is as attractive to birds as food, and some come more readily to it, either to drink or bathe, than to a bird table. A water container of any size will entice birds, from a small bird bath to a properly dug garden pond. After heavy rain when puddles have formed in the road or on the footpath, it is easy to see how keen birds are on water. This is particularly true in summer and in dry regions; such a puddle can provide great scope for photography. Sometimes it is necessary to act quickly before the pool dries up, but by putting up a hide about 5 metres (approx: 5 yards) from it and providing a fallen branch with a 300 mm lens, you can get some interesting pictures.

Water in the garden

More permanent, though possibly more conservative in forms of the species likely to come, is a regular supply of water that can be created in your own garden. One of the easiest bird baths to make is out of an upturned dustbin lid which can be sunk into the ground. Cover its edges with turf to create a nice little pond. This can remain quite shallow and will attract a large number of birds. Birds will also come to water butts when there is no other source of water.

Bird baths can be plain or ornamental, on a pedestal or on the ground. All these small types are liable to ice over in very cold weather; this can be overcome by putting an electric light bulb in a pedestal-type bath which, if left on overnight in freezing conditions, should prevent ice from forming. Small baths get dirty quickly so it is necessary to clean them regularly when filling them up.

Construction of a small pond

The addition of a larger pond to a garden is more of a pull to birds especially in places where water is scarce. As long as there is always water in it. Do not choose a confined situation as too much cover encourages cats to lie in ambush, and also prevents the sun from warming the water. The most simple way to make a pond is to dig a hole; line it with plastic sheeting and cover over the edges with turf to make it look natural, then fill it with water. A pond of this kind should last quite a long time provided nothing is put into it which is likely to cause a leak. To avoid stagnation the water should be changed frequently.

There must be a sloping edge from the bank on one side and a

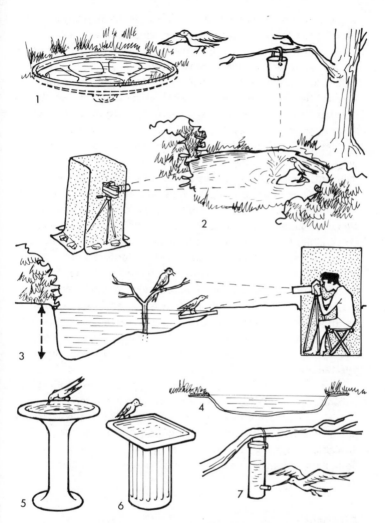

Bird baths and small ponds. **1** An upturned dustbin lid makes an excellent small birdbath. **2** A leaking bucket into a small pond acts as a great attraction to birds. **3** A self-made garden pond of concrete or polythene with a deep area of over 2 ft 6 in which will not freeze in winter. Small fish can therefore live all the year round. The shallow area with a paving stone is ideal for birds to bath from. A perch, too, encourages them to come down. **4** A small self-made or purchased fibreglass pond. **5**. Circular pedestal bird bath. **6** Rectangular tray on dustbin with water. **7** Water and sugar solution suitable for humming birds.

shallow area of water by it so the birds have a safe place to bathe. They have a fear of drowning in deep water and will be nervous if there is nowhere for them to come to. A paving stone just under the surface is ideal for this purpose.

If fish are kept in your pond in order to attract fish-eaters like herons, the pond must have a depth of about 2 ft to prevent it from freezing even in severe weather, thereby enabling the fish to live.

A good selection of plants can be grown round the edge to form natural surroundings. They will also give you attractive backgrounds for your photographs.

With this sort of pond you are able to put your hide in a more or less permanent position. Dig it a little way into the ground so that the camera is at a lower level bringing the lens more towards the same eye-level as the birds. This gives you a better viewpoint as you will not be looking down on your subjects so much. Birds will soon come to use the pond and, as with other forms of luring, the supply of water must be constant. Some birds are easier to photograph at a pond, drinking, than they are at a bird table where they might hardly ever come. Pigeons are a good example of this, as they seem to drink a lot. Dripping water always attracts birds; the movement and perhaps the sound arouses their curiosity. A bucket with a hole in it, hung from a branch so that water drips into the pond is a simple and efficient way to try this out.

Once birds start coming regularly to your pond photographing can be undertaken in exactly the same way as at the table. Perches may be put up either near or over the water so that the birds can preen after their bath; these make good subjects. As the pond is available all the year round you can probably get good shots of both adult and juvenile birds showing the different plumages.

Bits bags

Another interesting seasonal activity is nest building. In spring birds are keenly on the lookout for suitable scraps for their nests. Having found a good source of materials a bird will return to it several times. By collecting suitable natural stuffs and hanging them in the garden in a net bag birds will soon start attacking it to extract the bits they want. Any of the following is suitable: feathers, rope, string, fur, cottonwool, sheep's wool, dried grass or dried moss. It is important to keep them dry and, if good weather is forecast, these materials can be spread on the ground to attract initial attention.

For photography they can be attached to branches and you can get pictures of the birds holding bits in their beaks. A longer lens, from 200 mm–400 mm is the most suitable to use here as opportunities may occur in different parts of the garden and you will need more freedom from your hide.

Callback

Naturally enough birds are attracted by the song of other birds especially if it is that of their own species. Hunters are always successful when they can imitate the call of their quarry.

Tape-recorded birdsong is often used as bait. Several difficulties are associated with this approach, one of which is obtaining a recording of the species you wish to photograph. You may have to record the birdsong yourself which means an additional set of equipment and a lot of time. It is against copyright law to tape prerecorded material from records.

All that is needed in the field is a lightweight cassette recorder which is quite adequate if the volume can be turned up sufficiently. The quality does not have to be perfect so long as it is recognizable and not too distorted. Having got one suitable recording it is best to repeat it several times (by use of another tape recorder) so that you have several minutes of the call and can therefore leave the recorder on without having to change the controls.

The success or failure of this technique depends to some degree on the state of the bird you are attempting to call down. The best time of year when most of your work can de done, is the early part of spring when courtship is taking place between birds. Birdsong is vital in attracting a mate or defending a territory, so during the breeding season when things are happening very quickly callback can be most successful.

Some birds are very responsive to this form of lure; other species react very little or not at all. Still others may have mated and become disinterested in other offers, but the keen responses (often from territorial males) can be so intense that the birds try to destroy the speaker of the tape recorder in an effort to root out the intruder. Some responses can begin like this and then tail off quite quickly which does not give you much time to take photographs. This field has great potential and, in some avenues, is still unexplored. Lightweight recording equipment has made this relatively new branch of photography accessible to everyone. Caution however is as important here as anywhere else, as calling birds over too often may expose them to undue stress, and upset the natural breeding cycle. It has been shown with some species, however, that once a male responding to a tape recorder has found a natural mate this bond will overrule the recorder on future occasions.

It may not always be possible to draw birds out of thick cover as different families react differently depending on how territorial they are and what size territories they have etc.

When a bird does respond it is intent on finding the source of the song and may ignore you and your camera. Consequently it is not always necessary to use a hide as it is possible to have a songbird at 20 ft away, without one. The tape recorder can be placed by what is hoped to be a suitable perch and with luck the bird will land on it and sing to the recorder. In this situation use a longer focal length lens of 400 mm–500 mm to be able to cover other prospective perches too. Sometimes an even longer lens can be recommended but these are expensive and harder to use and not advisable to start with. Remote control can also produce results by using a convenient branch and so enabling a shorter length lens to be used and allowing you to be much further away. This can be great fun for one shot, but the bird may not return to the same place after the inevitable disturbance caused by winding on the film in the camera. In similar situations a hide can probably be used to greater effect.

To get the best out of callback, consistent observation of regular natural perches and notes of the weather conditions, to see when they are most used, should enable you to set up a hide with a tape recorder and lure the bird to the observed perch.

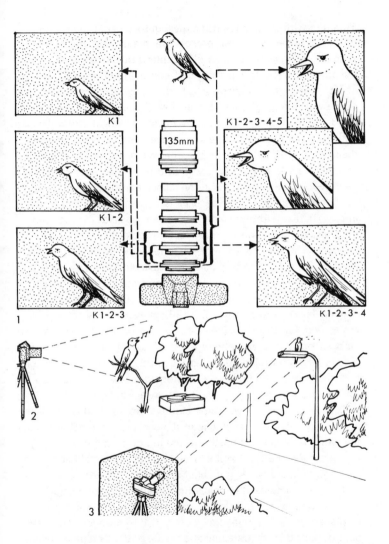

1 The effect of using different extension tubes on the image size of a bird. The closer you get to the bird the more extension you need and the larger the image size is. **2** Using a perch and a tape recorder to call a bird over. **3** Photographing a bird on a natural song post.

Mirrors

Together with song, birds use a great variety of display postures to attract a mate and deter prospective mates and rivals. This is normally difficult to show in photographs but by using a mirror it becomes possible to have the bird displaying on a perch of your choice. The sight of a displaying bird is of great interest to another bird even though it may be its own reflection in a mirror or window, and is usually enough to cause display or attack. Robins and wagtails particularly, tend to react with reflected images of themselves. This activity has been known to cause the death of a number of birds when they have battered themselves to death on a window by repeated attacks at the reflected image.

Therefore great care must be exercised with introducing a mirror into a bird's territory since any harm caused to the bird is unforgivable. As soon as the situation looks harmful it must be removed. The mirror does not have to be large but must be close to the bird, though it can be placed at ground level or at a convenient working height. Some birds display to wing mirrors on cars. I have watched this many times and wondered if this time lost while displaying has had any effect on the breeding success of the birds concerned, but this does not seem to have been the case. As with callback one can obtain photographs without the use of a hide and by using long focal length lenses. However, if you have a particular bird displaying regularly in a territory it is perfectly possible to introduce a hide and use a shorter focal length lens to obtain very satisfactory images. Some birds hide and appear frightened at the sight of a rival, and in such circumstances it is much better to take the mirror right away at once. Be sure to put the mirror somewhere in the species' natural habitat. This also applies to callback as the end result should be as authentic as possible. Otherwise, you may end up with pictures of birds in quite unnatural surroundings.

Another display response can come from a dead specimen which, if placed in an upright position off the ground, can cause considerable display. Care must be exercised in this form of baiting, and it must be remembered that it is strictly illegal to wilfully kill any birds as laid down in Britain by the Protection of Birds Act 1954.

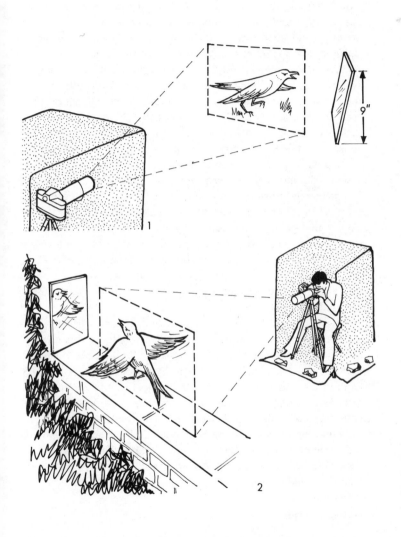

1–2 Using a mirror to attract a bird into displaying in front of it.

Birds and other animals

Concentrations of birds can easily be attracted by the regular scattering of food over an area of exposed ground. Large flocks of starlings and sparrows tend to congregate round farms, as do collared doves (*Streptopelis decaocto*) whose numbers are greatly increasing in some parts of Britain, and now beginning to breed in N America. These birds come for the animal foodstuffs that are present wherever there is livestock around. Anything spilt or left in feeding troughs will not go unnoticed. Finches, rooks and jackdaws come down for all food as well as hay; jackdaws and rooks are after the mineral-rich cake or nuts. This often leads to photogenic fights between individuals. Starlings look for any insects around the animals and their droppings. They and jackdaws tend to sit on the animals they associate with, especially pigs, which gives you excellent photographs throughout the year. You cannot get close enough in the open with your camera to get good results, so ask the farmer's permission to pose as the animal feeder. Sometimes birds land as soon as the food is out of the bag, but if you stop for a minute, or look round, they are all in the air again. Birds know exactly what the normal routine is and notice anything different.

Getting pictures of starlings perched on the backs of cattle was surprisingly more successful; the problem was to get the cows to remain at the edge of the field long enough for the birds to land on them. The answer came one very hot August day when they were lying in the middle of the field playing host to a large number of flies. The starlings were there too snapping at the insects. As the cattle seemed somnolent I decided to take a chance and erect a hide right by them out in the field about 20 ft away. They showed little interest and stayed where they were after the hide was up. It took only five minutes and, after another five, starlings were back feeding on their heads.

Hides in fields

The main problem with erecting hides in fields where there are animals, especially cattle, is that their curiosity will immediately be aroused. First they surround you, then gradually move in to lick and pull at the guy ropes, pushing forward to rub on the posts of the hide. Their interest wanes only when they have trampled your hide completely flat! Pigs are not much better; trying to scare them away only makes them more curious. Any bird, knowing the normal pattern of events, is bound to be suspicious of this behaviour and will not come near as a result. You may have to put up the hide on the other side of the fence. Use rough old farm sacks which will be inconspicuous. Birds, however, usually know when someone is there, and are nervous as a result.

Birds on farmland

At harvest time flocks of birds come looking for spilt food, and a hide at the edge of a field often produces photographs of them perched on fence posts and pecking about on the ground. Game birds can be seen after harvest and members of the crow family are much in evidence.

During winter ploughing large numbers of gulls and other birds come after the worms and larvae turned over in the fresh soil. Ploughing gives you many opportunities for spectacular pictures and a morning sitting on the back of a tractor, although uncomfortable, is very exciting. Vibration and movement are a problem in this situation so use a fast shutter speed: 1/500–1/1000 second. However, because they trust the tractor birds may come very close and so enable you to use a standard 50 mm lens or even a wide angle 35 mm lens. This is quite easy to hold, even in one hand, and it is also possible to pre-focus the lens so that you do not have to look through the viewfinder. This can be tried out by using the focusing scale on your lens.

Rubbish/refuse tips disposal areas

Refuse tips provide good potential for the bird photographer, especially during winter. A common sight is gulls creating a moving white mass over the ugly pile of rubbish. Quite a few species may be seen, though in Britain the most numerous exploiter of these places is the blackheaded gull (*Larus rudibundus*).

This location does not need a long focal length lens to produce results. A standard lens on the camera can capture the whole feel of this frantic activity, and if it is possible to introduce a hide the birds will come very close to it. As there are safety rules at rubbish tips it is necessary to get permission before photographing.

Baiting with carrion

When initially introducing such food as a dead rabbit it is better to leave it with the white fur facing skywards. Sharp-eyed birds can pick this out easily and are attracted to the white object. Photographing birds of prey is much harder since they are extremely suspicious and keen-eyed, and will show immediate fright at anything unusual.

The locations are very different from the average garden, being in open countryside where larger birds hunt over vast areas.

Hides in open country

Introduction of a hide has to be done before your work starts in earnest. The hide must be very firm and stable, and merge well with the surroundings. The material must be absolutely tight so that nothing can flap or move. The bait, if small like a rabbit, is likely to be snatched away by the bird unless it is staked to the ground to prevent this. No photographs are going to be possible, otherwise.

If you can, find a location on a hillside near a tree to make use of available cover. A suitable hide can be made from stones with tufts of grass covering the top to add camouflage. Very little camera movement, if any, will be tolerated by most carrion eaters likely to come down to this sort of lure. It is therefore essential to be properly set up before any bird is likely to come within range.

As with other forms of baiting this is best attempted during the winter months when birds are not breeding. Never put down a lure to encourage predators where there is any possibility of other birds with nests, as clearly, this will have disastrous results. Give the location plenty of thought, and consider the background too, and the direction from which the sun will come.

Equipment

In any set up it is desirable to get as close to the subject as necessary to enable a satisfactory image size to be obtained through the viewfinder without being so close that you cannot see what is happening. In a garden where you have food containers and a bird table, the likely subjects to appear will be small birds of 4–5 inches high. Though these are the smallest visitors much larger birds may fly down, especially if you bait for a carrion eater, though this would be most unwise and irresponsible in your garden, because of the presence of smaller birds.

The standard lens on your camera does not give a very large image unless you are virtually next to the bird. This would allow little or no camera movement and the birds would be highly aware of you.

The right lens

Different lenses have different effects. A standard lens, 50 mm or the 35 mm format gives, effectively, a natural view. A wide angle lens (28 mm) gives a wider angle of view through the camera, and a telephoto lens a narrower angle.

Additionally, the shorter length of lens offers greater depth of field; though helpful in maintaining a sharp image with a moving subject, it can be a disadvantage when trying to separate a subject such as a bird from a detailed background. The picture can look cluttered and the subject merged with the scene beyond. With much longer lenses the depth of field considerably diminishes, and so makes focusing very critical. A long focal length lens with its smaller angular field can give the same sized image of an object from a more convenient working distance.

Standard and wide angle lenses also tend to give a distorted image if they are used too close to the subject, and the short range gives a disturbingly steep perspective to the picture. Very long telephoto lenses can have the reverse effect; they appear to compress the field and foreshorten the subject and its surroundings.

The best lenses for our purpose are, therefore, a 135 mm or 200 mm (or an intermediate focal length) as these give enough depth of field, adequate working range and so, good perspective. With these lenses the bird will stand out sharply against the background. Physically, the lenses are fairly short which makes them easy to carry around and use hand held when conditions permit.

Shooting distance

The distance from which you take your photograph is directly related to the focal length of the lens chosen, and the image size required in the finished photograph. This shooting distance becomes very critical as you get closer to your subject and the subject consequently grows in the viewfinder. The closer the subject the smaller the aperture you need to allow sufficient field depth for the whole subject to appear sharp. But the chosen *f* stop is also determined by the film speed, light conditions, and any movement in the subject.

Image size

The choice of image size is, finally, a personal one, but it must be arrived at after some thought, and not just by chance. Any photograph, not only of birds, must be taken for a reason. With birds this could be an illustration of feeding, courtship or other activity, a particular close-up to show the head, feet or eye or simply a record of the species.

The assumption is that a straightforward record is required. In general the correct form this should take has already been stipulated and illustrated by many nature photographers. The bird should be shown with enough of its surroundings to depict its habitat, and should be in sharp focus from the bottom of the frame through to its tail. Although this is very much a standard approach it is not something that is always possible especially in a baiting situation where there may not be as much control and pre-dictability over the subject as there usually is at the nest.

Many good photographs have been taken through an out-of-focus foreground though this more often than not detracts from a picture rather than adds to it. Nevertheless it is a good thing to carry an idea around even if it is not always possible to achieve it. Invariably, even when the long focus lens is used at its minimum focus it will still make the bird too small in the viewfinder. This can be overcome with extension tubes.

Hides

For a bird to carry on its normal activities in its natural surroundings it is vital not to disturb it. Unfortunately, man is, by nature, clumsy, and has many habits which drive birds away (shooting for instance). However well-meaning you may be, you will never get very close to a wild bird without causing it stress to some degree.

Therefore a blind, or hide, as it is called in Britain, is the best piece of equipment to introduce into the vicinity of a bird that will accept it as part of the landscape.

Basic requirements

These hides can be large or small, permanent or portable. The bird photographer needs something that is light enough to be carried over reasonable distances in rough country and stable enough not to be blown away by the wind once it is put up.

All hides vary depending on the uses to which they are put. Basically they all stem from a standard design.

Standard hide construction

A standard hide is upright in shape with four sides and a square flat roof. It is big enough to hold a photographer and his equipment and to enable him to sit down comfortably. This last point is important as it can ruin a photograph if you become cramped and are not balanced and relaxed at the vital moment.

Standard measurements are shown in the diagram with suggested arrangements of viewing slits, camera holes and entrances.

Poles can be metal, wooden or plastic but should have some form of height adjustment on them all so that the hide can be level on a

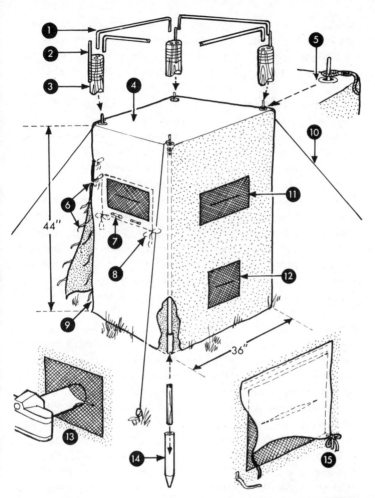

A basic hide for bird photography. **1** Metal rods. **2** Metal spike. **3** Top of wooden hide pole. **4** Canvas covering for framework, which should be a dark colour. **5** Brass ring set into canvas. **6** Material ties to secure entrance. **7** Safety pins to hold down gauze netting. **8** Material ties to secure flap openings. **9** Entrance and exit. **10** Guy ropes (only really essential in strong winds). **11** Camera opening through gauze or sacking. **12** Lower view point opening. **13** Camera inserted in opening. **14** Metal tubes for penetration into the ground (tapered wood posts will do). **15** Internal flap for covering gauze when opening is not in use.

hillside, or erected at half-height when necessary. Frame works should be kept simple in design so that they can put up quickly but still be firm enough not to be blown over by the wind. Usually guy ropes are quite adequate and can make a hide much simpler to construct and lighter to carry.

A complete framework welded so that all the pieces fit easily together, can make the hide heavy and cumbersome to carry around, but undoubtedly gives it strength. This ensures that there are no guy ropes to get in the way of the lens, and that the whole hide can be moved forward and back from within and the photographer does not have to reappear to make any moves.

The canvas need not be too heavy though it must be lightproof. If the sun is behind it so that your outline shows through the material, birds will instantly notice you and fly off. The colour can be varied, although darker shades are best. Remember that hides are not only for camouflage so that birds do not see you, but must merge well with the countryside so that other people cannot see it easily either. For example, never put up a hide in view of any road as this is asking for trouble, both for yourself and the bird. Materials mostly come in single colours but it takes only a few minutes to paint black spots or green and brown streaks to break the visual effect. Openings should be at a convenient height for seeing out of, and for the lens to emerge from. At the front of my own hide I have two openings, one much lower than the other, so that it is always possible to take a lower angle on a subject—particularly one nesting on the ground. If you look down on your subject too much you cannot get a good impression of the bird's appearance. A low viewpoint makes them much more impressive.

Safety pins are essential for pinning back flaps, and also to pin material to the part of the hide that is attached to the lens. It is advisable to have flaps that tie back over the openings as these do not make any noise. Once undone, you can then pin across the opening a suitably camouflaged or dark bit of netting that can be seen through without the subject being able to see you. I put a large piece of netting round the lens and pin it tightly to the inside of the canvas so that just the lens protrudes a little. This way the bird can see only the lens and the photographer can see through the netting or look at tte subject through the lens.

Introduction to a nest

All species, wherever in the world they nest, are naturally wild and suspicious of anything that might threaten them. The sudden introduction of a large object which is your hide, is certain to make any bird nervous so take great care. In Britain it is illegal to disturb some nesting species without a licence (*see* Appendix).

It is possible to photograph some birds without using a hide at all; colonial seabirds are a good example as many of them carry on their normal activities oblivious to the proximity of an onlooker, though there are always exceptions. Individuals of the same species can vary as greatly as do human beings, so even some of the apparently easy subjects need careful introduction to the hide. Great satisfaction can be gained from bringing a complete hide close to a nest without any apparent notice having been taken. In practice the bird always notices, and it is only when an action has been accepted that a resumption of normal activity continues. When undertaking anything near a nest it is vital to establish that this has, in fact, happened.

Moving a hide up open country

Birds nesting in the open are used to seeing a flat expanse with a distant horizon. The intrusion of a person or object can be seen from a long way off, so to photograph such a bird with a clear view, you must introduce the hide at the horizon first even if this is 200x or more. Try to place it near a tree so that it does not stand out by itself too much. Sometimes you may find that starting with the hide at half-height or almost hidden is the only way to make the bird accept it. By distant observation you can see the best direction from which the hide should approach the nest. The bird may sit in a favourite position and the angle of the sun is all important.

Make sure the bird accepts your hide. If it has it will soon return to its nest. The following day try moving the hide a quarter of the distance towards the nest. Check that the bird still accepts it and leave it for another day. If all goes well move it another quarter the next day, and a quarter the day after that. The hide will now look big to the bird which has come to trust it. After another day the hide can be moved about half of the remaining distance between it and the bird, might now be approaching 10x. The same afternoon try moving it again to 5x, and make sure the bird has not become frightened. If this is accepted, the next day the hide can be moved even closer to the working distance and left for the bird to build up its trust in it. On 'Day 7' after your first introduction the camera can be taken too. Up until this time the bird has been carefully watching each step. You are observed coming and going. Once you come to stay with your camera the bird will see no one leave. It is therefore essential that someone accompanies you to see you in, so that they can leave when you are ready in the hide to take photographs. With many birds this action is vital to trick them into believing that the danger which came has gone away. It is also imperative for someone to come out to the hide when you are ready to leave. If you suddenly emerge from the hide, in which the bird has built up so much trust, you will almost certainly destroy its confidence.

Certain members of the crow family can, it seems, count up to three. So with two people coming they expect two to leave. A way round this is for the assistant to carry at arms length a large overcoat when he leaves, giving the impression of two people walking. During the introduction it cannot be emphasized too much that the photographer must be prepared to withdraw at any stage. The bird should always return to the nest either to feed or incubate eggs within half an hour. If not then something is wrong. The bird can be left a little longer in warm weather. However, if eggs or young are exposed to direct sunlight or pouring rain and cold wind, they can quickly die. Always be fully aware of the possible result of your actions; if a long time passes and the bird has not returned you must pull down the hide and retreat, to enable it to come back. Only then can you start all over again, although it is better to look for another bird to photograph. Some birds are extremely difficult and are consequently best left alone. Make sure your hide does not cast a shadow that interferes with your subject. Overcome this by not going in too close and by keeping its height to a minimum. Conceal it in or against existing bushes or shrubs. If it is too tall to match the surrounding

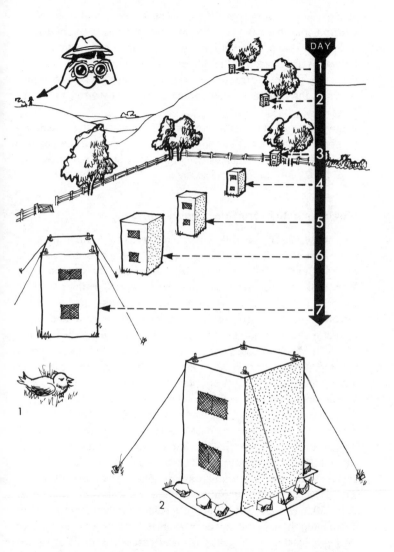

1 Introducing a hide to a nesting bird in open country, each stage being done on separate days; and each stage being carefully observed from a distance with binoculars. **2** Securing a hide in the open is very important. If you have one made, extra canvas at the bottom is very useful to put stones on, to stop the whole hide flapping and being blown away.

63

vegetation do not be put off by having to dig a foot or so down into the soil; this can also give you an improved viewpoint if the nest is low down. Another important point is to make sure that the hide does not block any flight lines that the birds regularly use into the nest. Careful observation will again tell you from which direction the parents usually approach, whether walking or on the wing.

If any livestock are in the area and likely to eat and eventually trample the hide, put a strong fence round it. Protect the nest too with a fence for any animals coming to look at the hide may well tread on the nest in the process.

Moving a hide in confined vegetation

Nest photography is difficult when the nest is built in open woodland or thick cover. For this reason many nests that you find or are shown, will prove to be impossible for photography. Numerous species have typical nesting sites such as the branch of a special tree or bush or by the foot of a certain sapling etc. Often for photographic purposes it is desirable to show a bird in as natural a situation as possible: Some sites may look too cluttered with vegetation almost concealing the subject. You must accept the fact that some nests that you find are unsuitable for photography, but as some species only ever nest in thick cover to photograph them successfully can be a challenge.

The cover that conceals the nest can be useful in concealing the hide too. Having found the nest make sure that it remains hidden. Be careful not to make a path to it through the vegetation as it will attract attention from both people and predators.

The time it takes to introduce a hide into a woodland or similar setting can be shorter than that for more open sites. Build the hide about 30 ft away so that the adults feeding and flying by can see it. By moving it half the distance every 24 hours you will be at working distance in 3 days. In many cases it is difficult to see whether or not the bird has returned to a nest, but a twig or piece of vegetation placed so that the bird cannot return without moving it, will soon indicate if it has been back. In some cases there may be no clear direction in which to move the hide forward. In dense cover this can cause considerable flattening of the surrounding plant life and should be avoided.

When working in thick cover like this it would be easy to creep up on the bird and surprise it. But to do so causes considerable alarm and if repeated can make the adult desert its nest. Therefore make sufficient noise to warn the bird of your approach so that it knows in good time and can prepare to leave the nest. Some water birds cover their eggs with weed when hearing danger coming; this not only conceals the eggs from hungry eyes in the sky, but also keeps them warm.

Some birds which nest in confined spaces, or those in the garden that are used to seeing human beings will only be slightly nervous at the sudden introduction of a hide. After 24 hours they are accustomed to it and can be photographed. Only attempt this with the commoner trusting birds that are familiar round your garden, since this sort of disturbance by a new clutch of eggs can frighten the bird enough to prevent it returning before the eggs go cold. It is therefore better to attempt this at a nest where the adults are feeding eager young. All birds differ, so always give yourself as much time as possible when getting close to a nest.

Building a hide in front of the bird

Where there is no room to move in any one direction it becomes necessary to build the hide up by degrees over the same sort of time scale that it takes to move it forward.

The fundamental difference between this approach and others is that you have to work very close to the nest right from the start. Time is all important and each stage must be completed as fast as possible so as not to keep the bird off the nest for any longer than 20–30 minutes at a time. Direct disturbance of this nature must only be done in reasonable weather conditions, so that the eggs or young will not get wet, cold or too hot through being unprotected by their parents.

When a bird is surrounded by thick cover the first stage is simply to spread the canvas on the ground where the hide will eventually stand. Lay it down, camouflaging it with available vegetation to hide it and prevent it from moving. After half-an-hour see if the bird has returned, and then go away for the rest of the day. The following day you can attempt to erect the hide to half its height, which is easily done if you have the kind with metal, wooden or plastic poles which join in the middle to make the full height. If your poles are all in one piece use four bits of wood to raise the canvas 2 ft off the ground giving the bird a definite change to get used to. Again, camouflage the canvas with vegetation which also weighs it down and prevents flapping. If this is accepted, try putting the hide to full height the next day. Remember that at any stage you must be prepared to give up for the well-being of the nest.

There are several situations when your conventional hide will not fit into your chosen location. Up trees you usually have to build a hide from available resources. Pieces of wood and planks can be gradually introduced over a period of time and these may be covered with wire netting over which suitably coloured hessian can be fastened. The wire netting will ensure that nothing flaps or moves. If necessary a simple block and tackle can be used to raise or lower the hide. The end result may not look conventional but as long as the bird accepts it and it is comfortable for you to work inside for long periods of time, almost anything will do.

Hides over water

Birds nesting on the water or in reeds either mean getting wet when photographing them actually in the water, or more desirably, building a hide or platform with the floor just above the surface. Pockets in the sides of the hide are invaluable for storing things that would otherwise end up in the water. Where no floor for the hide is possible, a gadget bag hung from the tripod adds stability.

A wood or metal platform can be built which may be 'moved up' as if on land, introduction to the nest taking four or five days depending on the species. In the final move it is essential to be sure the whole structure is firm, as any movement due to an unsteady floor will produce unsharp photographs.

If you build a platform larger than the base of the hide the conventional hide structure can then be wired onto it and moved slightly in any direction if you wish to change your viewpoint after

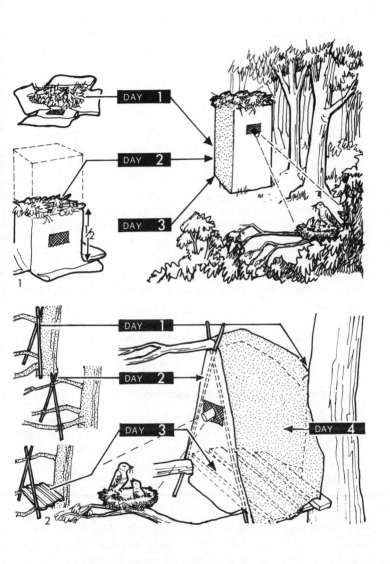

1 Introducing a hide in cover like the depths of a wood. Each stage takes a day. **2** Building a hide in a tree, each stage taking a day, as above. Care must be taken to make sure each stage is accepted by the birds.

67

the base is firmly in position. Waders are usually essential for moving about with equipment in water, as the additional weight often takes you further into the muddy bottom than standing there without it.

Dummy lenses and flash heads

Even after the hide has been introduced and accepted, it can happen that the introduction of the lens can make the subject very nervous. The same is true for flash equipment, but this is easily overcome by the use of dummies. An old bottle placed through the lens opening simulates a lens and can be left in the hide whenever it is not in use, giving the bird something to look at. It will soon get used to the bottle end, and will not stare nervously at your lens when you first start photographing.

A similar substitute can be made for flash heads, since, when introduced near the nest it takes a day or so for the bird to become accustomed to them. If they are left out for this length of time they get damp and do not function correctly. Therefore, a wooden or similar, dummy can be left out permanently in position. Small pieces of silver foil can be put on these dummies, facing the nest so that highlights too, can be accepted.

Procedures within the hide—equipment

In order to cause the bird as little disturbance as possible when entering the hide, you must be organized to set up the camera and arrange everything around you, as quickly as possible. Make sure that you can operate comfortably in the hide with the minimum of movement.

The best lens for this kind of work is a 135mm lens on a 35mm format SLR. The size of the bird and the size you want it in the frame must also be taken into consideration. With most small or medium sized birds 6ft is an average distance, and so some extension in the form of a tube or bellows will be needed.

In concealed locations flashlight is necessary; this is easy to introduce if dummies are used first. The final move of the hide is extremely important as the flaps will restrict the position for the

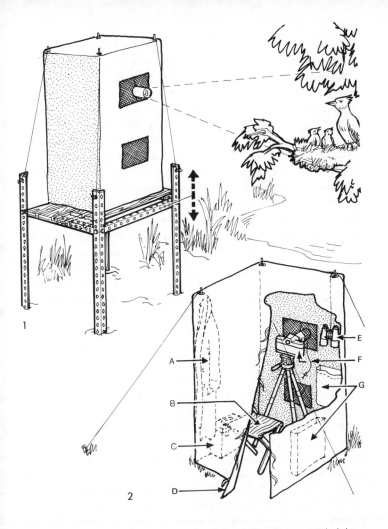

1 Platform hide, made from angle iron so that this can be at any height—particularly useful over water when the floor can be just above the surface. **2** Useful points concerning the interior of a hide. **A** Hang coat up in the corner on hook or butterfly nut if it is a frame hide. **B** Canvas collapsible stool—very important to sit on something comfortable. **C** Camera case. **D** Entrance to hide. **E** Binoculars are useful for watching your subject when it is some way off. **F** Cable release for camera eliminates camera shake. **G** Pockets sewn into the sides of the hide. These are very useful—especially over water—for holding notebooks, spare film etc.

camera lens. View the scene through the lens before making your move, and work out the best angle and position for the camera.

After this the hide can be moved easily. Once decided, the camera position must remain fixed, as any movement on its part will definitely expose the bird to undue stress.

Try using a tripod with a wide spread as this makes it firm for the camera and more comfortable for your feet. Keep the head well oiled so that there is no risk of squeaking which upsets the bird.

The camera position should be such that not too much of the lens emerges from the hide. If you have to move it when the bird is in the vicinity it will be less noticeable. A gauze netting with a slit for the lens can be pinned to the canvas round the opening on the front of the hide so that only the lens is visible from outside. The gauze can be left permanently there and the bottle substituted each time you leave.

Layout within the hide should be kept simple. Be sure to carry everything you are likely to need in one trip; this cuts down the disturbance time and is necessary if long distances are involved. To save time when in the area of a nest have the camera ready on the tripod and carry this over your shoulder. As soon as you enter the hide remove the dummy lens and replace the camera, adjusting the tripod legs. This can be a very quick operation. Seating is important, and a simple canvas stool is perfect as it is comfortable and easy to carry. Some gadget bags double as seats which is a great space saver. If long periods of more than 5 or 6 hours in the hide are anticipated, a back support is welcome. Under no circumstances must you touch, or lean on, the hide from the inside as this is a sure giveaway of its occupation. If possible leave a garden-seat with a back permanently in the hide to save carrying it around. I sometimes sit on a piece of foam rubber on an upturned bucket. I find the bucket very useful for carrying extras like food and flask.

On entering the hide lay out everything you are likely to need; complete the arrangements that make any noise. Place the camera case and gadget bag to one side so that they can be opened easily. For instance, film can be extracted from the makers' boxes and placed so that it is easily accessible. The best discipline of all is to have a definite place for everything, even a spare camera bush

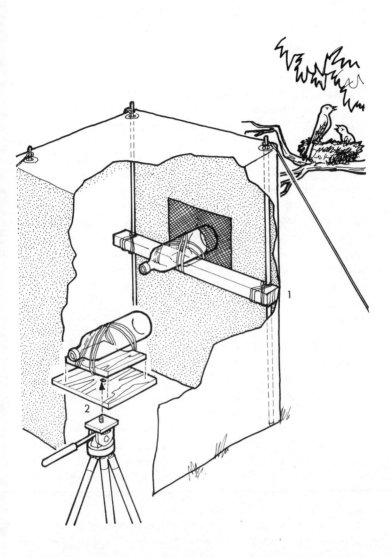

Inserting an empty bottle as a dummy lens in a hide, either by using the hide itself or by making something that fits onto your tripod. If you can leave your tripod in the hide, then the latter method will allow a very quick substitution of the real lens.

screw. By knowing where all the extras are you can go straight to them in your gadget bag or camera case without wasting any time when something is starting to happen outside.

Before settling down inside the hide put the flash, if being used, in place of the dummies. Always make sure that the batteries are fairly new or, if not, that you have spares with you. If using a rechargeable battery check the previous night that it is fully charged. When putting leads in from the camera to the flashes and their adaptors, make sure the joins are firm. A socket can easily be dislodged especially if a bird lands on the connecting cable and pulls it out, so put tape round it to prevent this happening. Make sure the cables are not too loose and cannot fall in front of the lens or the subject, which, if too near the lens cannot always be seen until it is too late. Tape and string are always useful. A piece of tape stuck to the back of the camera can be used to write details of the film you have loaded. If you require both colour and black and white, a second camera body is the answer if you are lucky enough to have two. If you do not, then taking a few shots on one film, noting the number taken, winding the film back to just before number one and then removing it from the camera, can enable you to take both. This can be a risky process. Be careful not to wind the film right back into the cassette as once in, it cannot be pulled out again. Remember to write on the leader of the film the number of shots exposed.

Reloading the film and winding it forwards again needs to be done so that no light enters the lens to fog the film. The best way to do this is to put the lens cap on and shield the lens with your coat; set the lens to the smallest aperture and the camera to the fastest speed and keep 'exposing' and winding on until you make the right number. Another disadvantage of this method is that sometimes winding the film in and out of the cassette can cause surface scratches on the emulsion.

It is always useful to have a variety of lenses in the hide. A standard and/or wide-angle lens can be used to photograph the habitat and perhaps the actual nest. It can pay off as sometimes, getting into or coming out of the hide, you see some beautiful skies well worth photographing. You may also see plants and other related material.

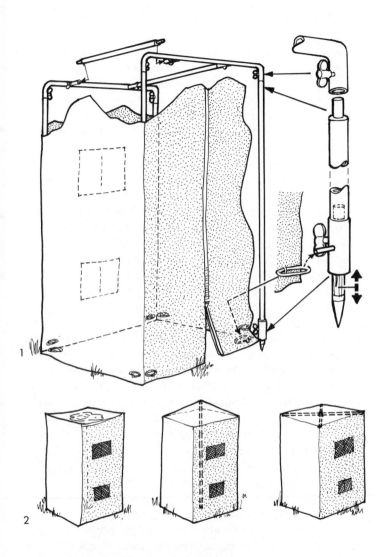

1 A strong framework hide made from alloy tubing. Very thick rubber bands can attach the canvas to the bottom of the framework, to keep it tight. Adjustable feet allow it to be erected on sloping ground. **2** Water often collects on the roof, causing it to drip and rot the canvas. So use a pole in the middle or cross pieces to prevent this.

Essential extras

Tape, string and rubber bands have many uses from attaching flash leads to simple stakes instead of elaborate tripods, to taping the cable release to the tripod handle so it does not knock against the tripod and make a noise.

Pins and safety pins are invaluable too, for pinning bits of the opening so you can see better, and using safety pins to hang up your coat inside the hide.

Screwdrivers have saved a loose lens mount in a hide for me, and penknives are always necessary sooner or later to cut an additional hole in your hide canvas. Back elements of a lens when being changed can easily get dust on them so be careful to prevent this. Have blower brushes, cleaning tissues and chamois leather. Chamois leathers can be the only solution to a misting-up eyepiece or even front element of the lens.

Cable releases are a must, as hand shake is a serious risk and can be avoided. Always have an exposure meter, even with an automatic camera as this may go wrong just at the worst moment. Haze filters offer such good protection for no loss of light to a lens, that they should always be kept on a lens; they eliminate ultra-violet rays which might otherwise give a blue cast to a naturally lit scene. Yellow and red filters can be used in black and white work to increase contrast; red to darken a sky which makes clouds stand out, although green foliage can go very dark. Yellow also darkens blue skies but renders greens a light tone so is helpful in monochrome. With some colour films a blue cast is present especially with flash, so a weak yellow filter like a Kodak CC05Y or CC10Y can help to eliminate this bias. Spare batteries are always important for flash particularly, and also for the camera if you have a built-in meter or even a fully automatic one. Keep spares warm in your pocket as in cold weather small camera batteries can refuse to function. Flash leads and connectors are easily forgotten but spares take up little room. Always have plenty of film; to run out can be heartbreaking. A torch is also extremely useful at the end of the day when packing up in a dark hide. Also some TTL cameras rely on light from the sky to illuminate the reading. A hide may be too dark for this, so the torch comes in very well.

Binoculars are practically essential for watching before you arrive and are also useful in the hide. A notebook, too, is valuable as you should always write things down as they happen so that there is never any doubt; behaviour, exposure details etc. are all easily muddled when back home again. Use a pencil as this will write in damp conditions when ballpoint pens will not.

Take enough food to keep yourself going and drink only enough to satisfy you thirst or to keep warm. Put all your food in tea towels or cloth that does not make any noise like paper bags which should be avoided.

Clothing

Clothing is as important as your other equipment and needs to be just as functional. Basically one needs to be cool in summer and warm in winter. Clothes should be quiet so that when moving in a hide no rubbing noises can be heard from outside. Therefore, wear wool and cotton, and avoid synthetic materials. Large pockets are very useful for a small lens and extra film if you have a long way to walk. A notebook needs a pocket too. The ideal garment is a suitably camouflaged anorak or similar weatherproof jacket. Dark colours are preferable in the countryside, and make good camouflage even though you may feel rather hot in the summer.

A hat protects against the sun, and helps to break up your silhouette from a distance. It is helpful for observation and, along with a face mask, can conceal you against a hedge.

In colder weather wear mittens which leave your fingers free to operate the camera; small cigarette lighter handwarmers are invaluable on frosty days. Good walking boots must be worn when carrying equipment across hills and rocks, as they reduce the chances of slipping or overbalancing.

Motor vehicles as hides

Cars and other vehicles have become so numerous that many birds are almost oblivious of them. Frequently when driving one has excellent views of birds by the roadside, in fields or sitting on telegraph wires, and they are often quite trusting in laybys and picnic areas. There is great scope here for the photographer and, although it might sometimes be dangerous to yourself and other road users, with care and luck you can get good photographs. Birds in hedgerows, on telegraph wires and at the edge of fields may not be at all bothered by the slow approach of a car. They may also tolerate the car stopping, but nine times out of ten as soon as the engine is switched off they will be away. Unfortunately it is essential to stop and switch off the ignition as while it is running it causes vibration to both you and the camera. The only way to overcome this is to be ready with your equipment, view the subject through it, focus, all with the engine still on. With everything ready, switch off the engine and press the shutter as soon as the movement has died away. With luck the bird may remain long enough for you to get a satisfactory result. Even if it does fly away it may not go far and this can give you another chance. All this is easy if you see the subject in good time and have your equipment at the ready. One usually sees these good opportunities when going somewhere not at all related to taking photographs. It is therefore a good idea to keep all your equipment in a solid case that can be put in the car. With your equipment at hand, on seeing a likely subject, you can often slow down sufficiently to prepare your camera and lens with the car still moving. This is not a good idea in busy traffic! Generally however, you see the subject as you are passing which is too late to stop suddenly. Drive on by and almost out of sight before turning round. Prepare the camera and then drive slowly as before; stop and take the photograph. Often the bird may be on the wrong side of the road; it is much easier with a long lens to use the passenger window or even the rear passenger window rather than the driver's window. The manipulation of the camera is easy and made fairly steady.

With this kind of photography a longer lens is nearly always necessary. A 400 mm is very useful. Longer lenses can be used to advantage on smaller birds, though they are correspondingly more difficult to keep steady. The most important thing is to get the lens as rigid as possible, and this can be done in the following ways: supporting the lens on the rubber of the window frame, with the window wound right down, can produce sharp results with practice, though some sort of support on the window is much better. A bean bag, a polystyrene bag or even a cushion all help to

1 Using the car for photography. Make the most of the support from its seats and windows. **2** Using the car as a hide. A piece of canvas or sacking shut into the door can provide excellent cover.

give the lens support as there is a much larger area of lens touching the stabilizing platform. Another way is by using the rear passenger window frames, again with the window wound down, and the back of one of the front seats to support the camera as well as the lens. Although this can be extremely steady it is sometimes necessary to give additional support to lens or camera to bring it to the correct height. There is rarely time to do this. If you anticipate doing much of this type of work it is not difficult to mount a pan and tilt head on to the side of the window frame. By means of a quick release button screwed into the lens mount the camera can quickly be put on or removed. Finally, in some cars it is possible to get a tripod fitting to the floor of the car over the passenger seat and then mount the camera in a conventional way. Whatever method you adopt always use a cable release as this can eliminate handshake when pressing the shutter. In some situations a small air release is invaluable as both your hands may be steadying the camera and the shutter can then be fired with your mouth.

In car parks and laybys the same approach can be adopted, though of course here the engine will not be a problem. It may be possible to use a shorter focal length lens especially if you drape a piece of canvas over the window and treat it like the front of a hide.

Wait and see

This term must be taken literally. By placing a hide near possible feeding, bathing or roosting sites, there is a good chance of interesting pictures. The species that appear, and their numbers are always an unkown quantity. One of the most popular and rewarding forms of bird photography is done in tidal situations when the tide pushes wading birds up the beaches, and they are forced to roost on outcrops of rock while their feeding sands are covered by the sea. Good knowledge of local tides is essential to aviod getting wet, though this is an occupational hazard. Feeding-birds on the tideline make a challenging subject.

Siting a hide for this work can be difficult as it must be positioned where it remains dry and birds are in front of you when the tide does come in. It is best to enter the hide while the tide is still a

Wait and see hides, by the sea. **1**–**2** Waders brought in on the tide are a remarkable spectacle: **1** At low water the occasional bird may appear soon after you are in the hide. **2** By high tide, hardly any space remains for birds to sit. Careful research will tell you where the best places are.

long way off, and wait until it brings the birds up with it whereupon they will remain until the tide recedes enabling them to feed. Be prepared to wait until the tide has gone out far enough for the birds not to be alarmed by your re-emergence from your hide. Above all, never disturb them when they are roosting as this land may be the only safe place for them to go, and you may frighten them away permanently.

Any lens ranging from 135 mm–500 mm in focal length can be used from such a hide depending very much on how close the birds come to you. A tripod is again a 'must'; a jerky lens will certainly frighten birds. With the uncertainty of the subject you will have to pan to keep the bird in the viewfinder. This means having a larger piece of gauze pinned more loosely to the hide and attached to the lens. It is always advisable in any outside work to use a lens hood to prevent strong light flaring on the front of the lens. This hood is a nonmoving part of the lens so the end of the netting can be attached to it.

Setting up may have to be done quickly and it is advisable to be well practised. Set the tripod and camera up making sure it is level and pans from side to side, maintaining a level horizon. Then put up the hide over it, making sure it is firm and able to withstand wind, rain and possibly shallow tidal water. It is often easier to set the camera and hide up this way round. Once the hide is up make sure that you have enough room to pan both sides without getting the hide poles in frame too soon. Guy ropes in this situation often get in the way. Therefore some kind of framework hide is better. Always wear waders on the coast as these not only keep your feet dry, but if necessary you can kneel on wet sand and remain dry, while taking a photograph. The coast is not the only place to do this. Anywhere from a drinking pool, fish farm or popular migration spots can be rewarding, often producing the unexpected. In certain countries hides so placed at migration times attract the unwanted attention of shooting interests.

Flash

What is flash?

A high intensity light source of short duration is what is understood to be flashlight. This can be achieved by two methods: (i) by the use of flash bulbs and (ii) by electronic flash.

Flash creates great scope for the bird photographer giving successful photographs where none would be possible without.

Both methods produce light which matches daylight in colour quality, so there is no need to use a filter on the camera nor a special film, as is normally the case when using artificial light sources. Any daylight sensitive film can be used; all film is marked for daylight or tungsten artificial light on the film box when you buy it. It is possible to obtain a correction filter to make a tungsten film suitable for use in daylight, and vice versa, although in both cases there is effectively, some loss of film speed, particularly when filtering daylight type film for use in artificial light.

Flash bulbs

These create their flash by the very fast burning of an incandescent filament in an enclosed glass envelope filled with oxygen. They vary in size from approximately the equivalent of a car headlamp bulb to that of the normal electric light bulb used domestically, in the case of the most powerful type. Flash bulbs are easy to carry are relatively inexpensive and come in many different forms. The most simple are flash cubes which are not really suitable for bird photography. The main disadvantage of bulbs, which in many cases rules them out for use in photographing birds, is that they are expendable and have to be replaced after each shot. Consequently, they are fairly inexpensive which makes them attractive. However, used in any quantity and over a period of time, they soon become an expensive way to provide flash. An electronic unit costs more to buy, but is much cheaper to run.

Electronic flash

Electronic flash works by passing a large amount of electrical charge through an ionized gas in a clear tube. The intense illumination is produced for only a very brief instant—a far shorter period than that of a flash bulb. The slower type electronic unit discharges its flash within about 1/500 second, and some of the fastest automatic types may go up to 1/40 000 second in particular circumstances. Most portable units operate at around 1/500–1/1000 second in average conditions and at this sort of speed produce their maximum output of light. This is ideal for most bird subjects, as only when more specialized photographs of small birds in flight are wanted is it necessary to consider anything faster.

The ideal arrangement for bird photography is to use either one or two heads operating from a single power pack, or independently powered units. Portability is vital; so is ease in recharging or changing batteries.

Portable units come in many different sizes which bear a very approximate relation to the power output to be expected. They also vary in the number of flashes each will produce from a set of batteries. In addition, some have automatic control over the amount of light they discharge (auto or 'computer' flash).

An automatic flash unit can be programmed to give correct power output over a range of distances without making aperture adjustments for each situation. It does this by means of a sensor built into the front of the flash. As the light from the unit is reflected from the subject it is measured by the sensor and, when the subject has received sufficient for correct exposure at the aperture set, the unit automatically quenches the flash. The unit often indicates a choice of apertures that may be set for any given film speed, and shows on a dial the possible subject range within which the unit operates correctly. Because exposure control is achieved, in effect, by shortening the flash duration in particular circumstances this may be very short indeed, as with high ASA speed films the duration of the flash (for the same aperture) is much higher, so it might be thought that a high speed film was going to be ideal to improve the chances of getting movement-free pictures. Unfortunately high speed colour materials do not give

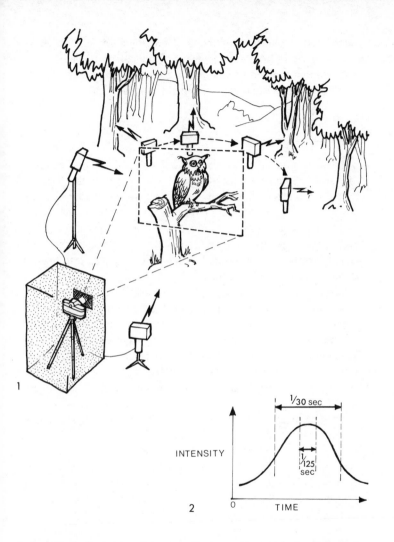

1 Open flash. By leaving the camera shutter open at night, multiple flash exposures can be made by moving round the background before (or just after) the subject appears. Then use the flash set up as you would normally. Provided it remains dark then nothing can interfere with the image. **2** A graph illustrating the length of time a disposable flash bulb takes to produce all its light. To obtain most of the light, a long shutter speed is necessary: if a shorter one is used, then only a proportion of the light is available for the exposure.

such good colour saturation and are more difficult to expose correctly. Apart from this there is a greater risk of 'ghosting' due to the fact that synchronization has to be at a setting of no more than 1/60 or 1/125 second with a normal focal plane shutter.

Synchronization

All flashes are fired by the closing of an electrical circuit and this is done by the camera through the lead coming from the flash gun. Cameras can have different types of flash sync setting, most SLR's have two; one for electronic (X) and another for bulbs (M). A flash bulb builds up its light intensity over a period of several milliseconds so the triggering on 'M' sync is arranged with a suitable delay so that the bulb is burning at its brightest when the camera shutter is fully open.

With cameras having focal plane shutters, flash bulbs must be used only with shutter speeds of 1/30 second or less. As the triggering and duration of electronic flash are much faster, the sync timing ('X' socket on your camera) is different and the flash takes place while the shutter is fully open in order to expose the whole frame. With most focal plane shutters the whole frame is only revealed at shutter speeds up to 1/60 second or, in some cases, 1/125 second.

Electronic flash guns emit a high pitched whine as they are charging and have a neon indicator which lights up when they are fully charged and ready for firing. The time this takes varies between 3 seconds–30 seconds depending on the condition of the batteries and the particular unit you are using. Always wait a second or so after the neon light has come on, to make sure the unit has really finished charging.

Exposure: computer

The exposure control method or computer flash method gives accurate exposure every time, but in practice works best only if most of the subject is in the same relatively flat plane. If the subject is small in the frame and seen against a large background then the background gets the correct amount of light, overexposing the subject. If this is a bird on a perch seen against a distant background then the flash may give off its maximum output trying to get a response from what is effectively out of its range. The very fast flash from a computer flash gun can be extremely useful for showing small birds using their wings or any other form of fast action. To exploit this characteristic in situations where it would not normally operate of its own accord, units can be cheated into thinking that they have given off the correct amount of light by putting a very small reflector in front of the light sensor. By doing this the flash is quenched extremely quickly thereby giving a very short duration flash but at the same time a very weak one. Because of this its use becomes limited as the flash heads have to be very close to the subject which, with birds, is not very practical. It also results in pictures with unnaturally dark backgrounds which, again, is difficult to overcome.

The only way to avoid an unacceptable background is to introduce something that can be lit separately by a similarly cheated flash so that both lights go off at the same speed and do not cause 'ghosting' by going off at different speeds. For common garden birds a background of white card or a cloth can be put up behind a perch, thereby making a background which will, and should be, out of focus and reasonably evenly lit. This can be done by using only one head (see black and white section: bluetit, *Panus caeruleus*). The shadow caused has fallen so that it is not evident on the background in the finished result.

It is not always desirable to use a flash gun in its computerized mode, as it is often necessary to use all the available power. Some units can be set to manual which overrides the computer and gives the maximum output with a flash duration of possibly 1/500 or 1/1000 second. If no manual setting is provided put a piece of thick tape across the light sensor so that it thinks no light is being reflected back, and therefore does not quench the output.

Exposure: manual

Most flash guns have no provision for varying the output, although with one or two models it is possible to select a half-power mode.

Like all forms of flash a constant light output is given each time the unit is fired. With manual units this is their maximum power. The speed may differ, depending on the unit, between 1/500–1/2000 second.

To determine the exposure a guide number can be used which is usually written on the flash by the manufacturer. Guide numbers give an indication of the relative light output from the flash when used with film of a given speed. The higher the number for the same film speed, the more powerful the flash. The guide number varies with the different ASA ratings of the film you use in your camera. To use the guide number to determine the aperture to set, you divide the distance of the flash from the subject for feet or meters and this gives you the aperture to use on the camera. So, for a flash unit with a guide number (in feet) of say, 80 with a particular film with the flash at 10 feet, you will need to set an aperture of f8.

When working close to your subject as you will with many birds, the flash may be at 4 ft and, again, using the same film and flash as above, you will be on $\frac{84}{4} = 21 = f21$ (in practice its nearest equivalent is f22). Experience will soon tell you if f22 is all right, or whether you have to move the flash a little nearer to get slightly greater exposure. You must be sure that the distance you set and the guide numbers quoted are in like terms, i.e. either feet or meters. It is more usual these days to quote the effective output of the flash unit in meters.

With more powerful flash guns you may have a guide number of say, 180; at 4ft an f stop of f45 will be necessary. Not many lenses go beyond f22 and f45 is two stops smaller than this. In such cases neutral density filters have to be used over the camera lens as they can absorb at least two stops of light, and are available in versions that absorb different amounts of light. Another alternative is to switch the flash to half power (if the outfit has this facility) but you will still have to use the equivalent of f32 and are therefore forced either to use a filter or to move the flash units further away. The latter course is probably better as lights too close to birds (at 3ft or less) can make them nervous.

Many people wonder if flashlight is harmful to birds, but it is generally accepted that it causes them no stress. If your subject is

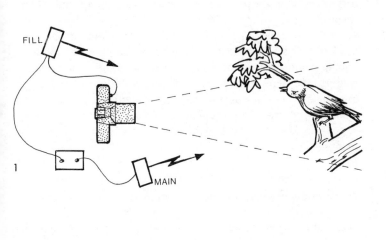

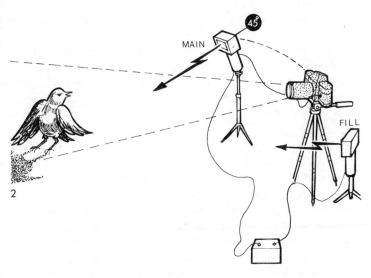

1–2 A basic set up for using two heads of flash, seen from above in **1** and from the side in **2**. The main lamp should be higher than the camera to represent the sun, so that it gives a realistic shadow.

staring at one of the flashes try not to expose it until it looks elsewhere. In the case of owls it might very momentarily blind them.

A flash meter provides an alternative method for determining exposure. This special form of light meter can plug into the flash unit and fire it from the subject position to give an accurate reading. They are very expensive and only really useful when using several flash units at a time—a situation that does not arise in most amateur work, so it is not worth spending your money this way. Experience is still the best method to give you some idea of what to expect.

Disposable or rechargeable batteries

Many of the smaller flash units are powered by penlight or similar batteries, and these give a useful number of flashes for each set. The magnesium alkaline type, although more expensive, give many more flashes per set and a fairly constant recycling time. The cheaper variety gives longer recycling times as the batteries are used up, which can be inconvenient. All penlight batteries are easily changed and are not too heavy to carry around which is a great asset. For the larger units there are three different types of battery in general use. The heaviest is the dry disposable battery that does not need recharging at all. This gives a very large number of flashes and can be used with cells that use more than one head. It is particularly useful in the field if there are no facilities for recharging the lighter nickel cadmium (Nicad) dry cell or the lead/acid accumulator wet cell.

Nickel cadmium rechargeable batteries are probably the most popular type in use for general flash photography. They can give up to 150 flashes per charge from the home power supply, and a fast recycling time. If looked after they should last a very long time. They must be recharged while being not in use after a week or so. Beyond this period a full charge of 12-16 hours may be necessary to bring the pack up to power. Being a dry cell they are excellent for travelling and though expensive, can be very easily replaced.

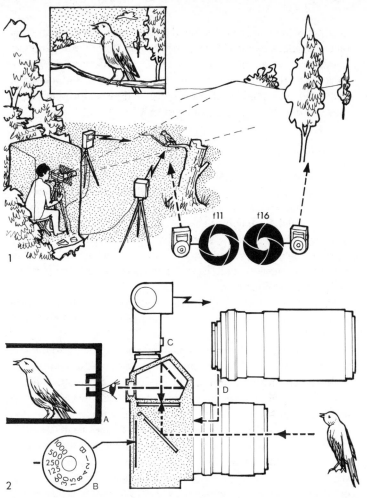

1 Balancing flash with daylight. If your subject is in shadow, then the reading will be less on this than the background. The flash can then be balanced. If both readings are the same, flash can be used on the bird, which could then make the background darker and the subject stand out.
2 The SLR camera viewing a bird. **A** Automatic metering through the lens tells you when the exposure is correct when the needle appears in the middle of the viewfinder. **B** The shutter speeds are set by a dial from 1 sec to 1/1000 sec. This is directly related to the emulsion that is on the film. **C** Computerized flashgun mounted by 'hot shoe' directly onto the top of the camera: this is only useful for fill in work. **D** Interchangeable lenses make SLR cameras very versatile. By changing lenses from a fixed position, correct image size can be obtained.

Lead/acid wet cell accumulators hold their charge much better and give considerably more flashes per charge than nickel cadmium. They also have an indicator on the side of the flash to show what level of charge remains. They must be kept charged, and topped up with distilled water. If left for long periods without being used, they can deteriorate and become useless.

Basic lighting

Why use an artificial light source at all? Some people believe that daylight gives all the light needed for photography, but there are several advantages in using flash. Each one solves a different problem. First, flash light is very strong and directional. Its strength enables a much smaller *f* stop to be used, thereby increasing the depth of field. When working close to a subject this is important and tremendously helpful. Care has to be taken so that the whole picture area is properly lit.

Second, it can arrest movement due to the brevity of the exposure. With small birds particularly, which are rarely still for long, this is very useful.

Third, flashlight can be used in areas so badly lit that photographs cannot be obtained in any other way. This is especially true at night, when creative lighting can produce a moonlight effect. A dense woodland or anywhere with thick cover nearly always needs additional light.

In any controlled situation it is possible to use flash on birds. Before you start work out what effect is best and how to achieve it. It is a reasonable assumption that all daytime flying birds should be shown in daylight. Any lighting must be made to look like sunlight or overcast skylight. Direct sunlight always creates a highlight area and a shadow area, though this can occur from any direction. Overcast skies produce a pleasant diffused light which is much nearer to being shadowless. For most colour photographs this weather is ideal; hard shadows can spoil a photograph. The beauty of daylight over flashlight is that it is completely even throughout any scene that you may want to photograph outside. Flashlight falls off very fast over distance so that it becomes easy to obtain well-lit subjects against dark backgrounds which for daytime birds

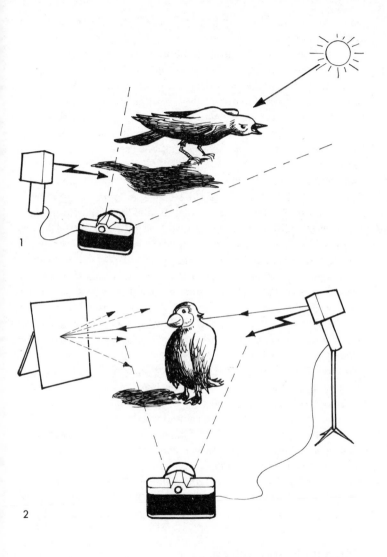

1 Use of fill in flash to prevent too heavy a shadow obliterating detail from the near side of the bird. **2** Using a white card, silver paper or a mirror as a reflector to bounce flashlight from one head to 'fill in' the shadow area it creates.

is unacceptable. This drawback prevents flash from being used in many situations.

So not only must backgrounds be controlled, but shadows too. Photographing people with photofloods, or even watching the formation of shadows on a face with a moving anglepoise light, can teach you a lot about the positioning of lights and the shadows they produce. With any flashlight photography you cannot see what effect the lighting has, so it is very important to remember what you do each time. You can learn a lot from experience.

Any bird subject has form and shape which should be shown in a photograph. One test will tell you that one light coming straight from the camera position gives such frontal lighting as to produce no impression of any modelling at all. The light must be held away to one side of the camera and immediately a shadow is apparent. If the light is then moved up the shadow will take on the type similar to that cast by the sun. But one light used like this cannot produce the same overall effect of the sun because the shadow it makes is far too black. Another light can then be used on the opposite side of the camera to the first light, and lower down, to shine so that the shadow, although still there, is reduced but with the detail still visible.

We now have a simple arrangement using two heads of flash for simulating bright sunlight. This is the basis of much photography at a nest and elsewhere, where this type of lighting has to be used.

When using two heads of the same power, the fill-in flash should be further away in order not to completely kill the shadow created by the first light. Alternatively its power can be reduced by placing a white handkerchief over it.

It is easy to see that the light will fall off quickly with this arrangement and will not illuminate the area any distance behind the bird unless there is a suitable background to catch the light.

Fill-in flash with sunlight

Flash can be used very successfully with a subject which is in mixed sunlight and shade, or has direct sunlight on it causing a hard shadow to one side or underneath it. When working in black

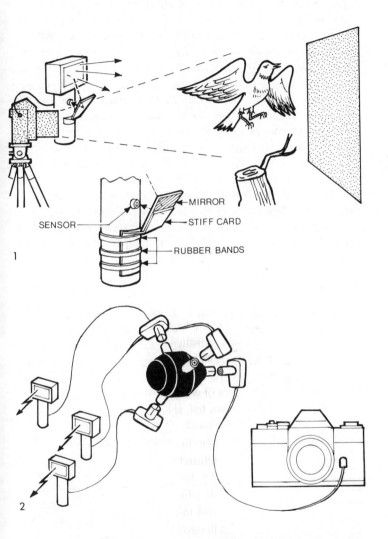

1 Cheating a computerized flashgun to give a very short duration flash. Either a mirror or a white card can be used. An artificial background can also be used to prevent a pitch black background. **2** Another way of connecting up many flash heads to make all fire simultaneously, by means of a three-way adaptor.

and white you can overcome this problem by slightly overexposing and under-developing the negative, so reducing the contrast of the original subject. In colour this is a somewhat more difficult problem since the film of lower speed and higher colour saturation tends to be high in contrast and therefore records very dark shadows in strong sunlight. Clearly it is desirable to soften these shadows in some way. With flash, placed so that it shines into the shadow area, 'filling it in', this shadow can be considerably reduced and can produce a very pleasing photograph. Typical situations where this occurs are in woods where dappling sun is all that filters through the trees onto the birds breeding there. Exposure here can be taken in the ordinary way, for the background, say 1/60 at $f11$, and then the flash can be placed at the correct distance to give approximately one stop less than this ($f8$) so as not to obliterate the shadow completely. Alternatively a computerized flash may sometimes be programmed to give the chosen f stop.

Reflectors

It is always possible to use one flash head and then a reflector to fill in the resulting shadow; effectively the main light then takes on the position of the sun and can be set to full power. Such a reflector can be used in many ways; it might consist of a sheet of white card; a white painted piece of wood or either of these two objects being covered by aluminium foil, shiny side up for a harder fill-in and matt side up for a softer result.

As with the main light source, the larger the surface area of the reflector the softer, more diffused light it will give. This is why portraits are often taken by bouncing flashlight off a white umbrella, producing shadows which are much kinder to the face. Clearly it is not practical to work like this in the field; because of the diffusion and because it has to travel further to get to the subject, the light becomes much weaker. So some of the advantages of the flash may be lost as a wider aperture will have to be used.

Applications—subject isolation

Walking through a thickly-treed wood on a bright sunny day, shafts

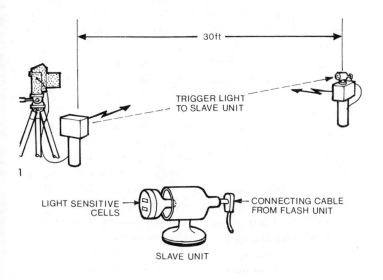

30ft

TRIGGER LIGHT
TO SLAVE UNIT

1

LIGHT SENSITIVE
CELLS

CONNECTING CABLE
FROM FLASH UNIT

SLAVE UNIT

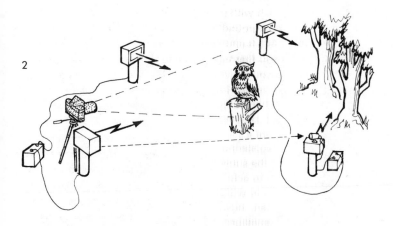

2

1 Using one flash to fire another simultaneously by means of a slave unit. The distance over which this will work depends on the power of the flash from the camera. **2** Using a slave unit on a typical subject. If two individual flashes were used, then each one would have its own slave unit. Theoretically any number of slave units can be fired by one flash, all simultaneously.

of sunlight come through the foliage highlighting the leaves and plants on the ground beneath them. Because of the general low light level in a shaded wood the sunlit objects stand out well in isolation.

Flashlight can act in exactly the same way on any subject, and in ordinary daylight and sunlight too if desired. A subject can be isolated by exposing it with stronger light than daylight, thereby rendering the background dark. We know that this is unacceptable on daytime flying birds, so must be avoided unless complete isolation against a black background is desired for specific reasons. Isolation of the subject is important and must be achieved by looking for suitable backgrounds. These can be placed and created close to the subject so that light from the main flash can fall on both. Alternatively a separate light can be used on the background; whatever it is, if both it and the subject are going to be evenly lit then it must be uncluttered in order not to compete visually with the subject thereby drawing attention away from it. There are, nevertheless, situations when either of these two possibilities will not be practical and the background is going to be a long way off and far too big to put lights on. We have already examined the application of flash with sunlight, and using it on a subject with a large daylight background is really much the same. If you are close to your subject at 5 ft and you want to shoot at f16 to get adequate depth of field, you first take a reading off the background. It may well be that this could give you a rather slow shutter speed of 1/30 or 1/15 second or less for f16. Setting the shutter for, say 1/15 second, the flashlit subject and the background will both be correctly exposed. However, the subject must not move during the exposure to prevent a secondary image caused by the existing light on the scene, registering on the film at such a relatively long exposure time. If the subject is in the shade and the background is not, this can help to achieve an even result. If the subject is not in shade or is evenly lit with the background it could be that flash is innecessary. It can, however, greatly lighten a photograph and bring it to life. Sometimes, in this latter case, it is better to give the flash one stop less than the background and subject meter reading (being the same) to avoid overexposure of the subject. This method can be used to get photographs of many birds against

Above   Little grebe *(Podiceps ruficolis)*
Taken from a platform over the water. Slow shutter speed in daylight.

Opposite, top   Dartford warbler *(Sylvia undata)*
This ground nesting bird can be difficult to see. The heather was held back to give a clear view. Two flash-heads had to be used for lighting.

Opposite, bottom   Dartford warbler *(Sylvia undata)*
On a perch used regularly as it approaches its nest. A 400 mm lens isolates the bird from the background.

Previous page   Blue tit *(Parus caeruleus)*
High speed flash using a single computerized unit with an artificial background behind the perch. Photographed near a feeding area in a garden.

Above Barn owl *(Tyto alba)* killed on the road.
This sort of photograph can have as much impact as one of a live bird. Taken in sunlight the effect is produced by printing in the background while enlarging. A wide-angle lens, 40 mm on 6 × 6 cm (2¼ × 2¼ in), provides good depth of field.

Opposite Starling *(Sternus vulgaris)* on a cow's head.
A fast shutter speed is necessary to prevent the constantly moving bird appearing unsharp—1/500 second, *f* 11 on high speed black-and-white film.

Opposite   Avocet *(Recurvirostra avosetta)*
Isolated by differential focus with a very long lens—100 mm (on 35 mm), and *above* showing bird photography applied to publicity. An effect that can be obtained by shading the print while enlarging. This has been used as a symbol by the Royal Society for the Protection of Birds and reproduced on carrier bags etc.

Above Black-headed gulls *(Larus ridibundus)*
Taken from the back of a tractor using a 35 mm lens on a 35 mm camera. Very uncomfortable shooting position but a common sight well worth recording!

Opposite House martins *(Delichon urbies)*
Collecting for migration. Taken from the ground with no hide. Watch out for regular locations that are used.

Above Bewick's swan *(Cygnus bewickii)*
The original was taken against the light with a 400 mm lens. This was printed from a line film intermediate stage, the 'sun' was added in the darkroom.

Opposite, top Herring gull *(Larus argentatus)*
Following a boat at sea. By panning with the bird it is possible to use a slower shutter speed and smaller aperture, 1/250 second f16.

Opposite, bottom Puffin *(Fratercula arctica)*
Waiting for the bird to fly into focus and stopping movement with a fast shutter speed 1/1000 second, f8, a 400 mm lens was used, hand-held.

Above   Spoonbill *(Platalea leucorodia)*
An unexpected opportunity at a 'wait and see' hide. Long lens—1000 mm.

Opposite, top   Coots *(Fulica atra)*
Fighting in territorial dispute. The film speed, being uprated by forced processing, allowed a shutter speed of 1/1000 second to be used with this 1000 mm lens whose maximum aperture was only *f* 11.

Opposite, bottom   Gannets *(Sulabassana)*
While photographing them in flight this shot of a fight was taken. This sort of un-expected occurrence makes bird photography so exciting.

Above A simple homemade hide covered with hessian sacks. This was used for photographing birds associated with farm animals.

Opposite Camouflage for observing and stalking birds. Gloves to cover the hands and a face mask to prevent the white showing up from a distance.

Overleaf Blue tits *(Parus caeruleus)*
The birds were photographed inside a nest box. A glass panel was built into the side of this nesting box and was continually covered until the time arrived for taking pictures. Only flash would allow sufficient depth of field at such close range.

natural backgrounds, though invariably the bird must be very still and many exposures may be wasted before a satisfactory result is achieved.

Multihead use

To emulate a bright sunny day two flash heads are used. These can be two similar small units at different distances, or at the same distance with one diffused to give a weaker light. The same is true for two headed units which run off the same battery. These are very convenient as they fire simultaneously from the one lead to the camera, but what if we want to use more than two heads, say three or four or even more?

Relatively few units have the facility of taking more than two heads from the same power pack though one or two of the more expensive portable sets do so. With these you can run three, four or more, off the same power source, but obviously you will get fewer firings before having to recharge. The normal arrangement now, for amateur use, is to set up with separate self-contained flash units.

I have stated a use for three flash heads, namely that of lighting a background as well as the subject; this can be possible for many birds, and a great help. It is not necessary to use expensive equipment for this. Any three flash units will do if you know how much power they give out. Connecting them together is probably the main problem. There are two ways of connecting three or more leads so that they all fire at the same time. The cheapest is to buy a two- or three-way adaptor, depending how many units you wish to use. This is a simple small junction by which several flash sync leads are routed into the single camera contact. The disadvantage of this set up is that often, especially working in thick vegetation, additional leads do get in the way of all the other equipment, and can creep into the camera frame remarkably easily. The actual connections can come out—and so have to be checked frequently to prove that they are still working. All this takes time but is easily avoided by taping each connection so that they cannot be pulled out. Experience has shown me that flash guns of different power used with leads of different lengths do not always work together. The other method of coupling flashes together is by using a slave unit.

Slave units

A slave unit is a light sensitive cell which connects to the camera end of a flash sync lead. It responds to the flash from another unit by instantaneously firing the flash to which it is connected. Provided the slave sensor is pointing at another flash, which is easy to arrange, it will work over a distance of 30 ft or more in some cases. Slave units are not particularly expensive; they cost the same as a small flash gun. Their convenience makes them highly attractive as there are no leads to get in your way.

With complicated set ups requiring many flash units, it is possible to fire any number by a single small flash from the unit connected to the camera sync contact. However, be quite sure they are securely pointing at the flash, so that birds cannot alight on them and upset the direction in which they are directed.

Night-time photography

Flash is extremely useful at night as without it no photography could be attempted on many natural species. The principles for using flash at night are exactly the same as using it in the day, though a black background is acceptable for nocturnal creatures since they are normally shrouded in darkness.

One of the biggest problems with working in the dark is trying to focus the camera satisfactorily. With many species you can use a dark red torch light at night, which can be permanently turned on. You can see your subject arrive and focus onto it. Under no circumstances must the light flicker as birds will not tolerate it. Use a heavy duty battery as it will not appreciably alter during several hours of use.

Many nocturnal species are completely silent, enabling them to catch their prey and preventing you from hearing their arrival. Visits to a nest may be infrequent, so there may be fewer photographic chances than with daytime birds.

In this situation it is possible to use flash bulbs. It may be the only

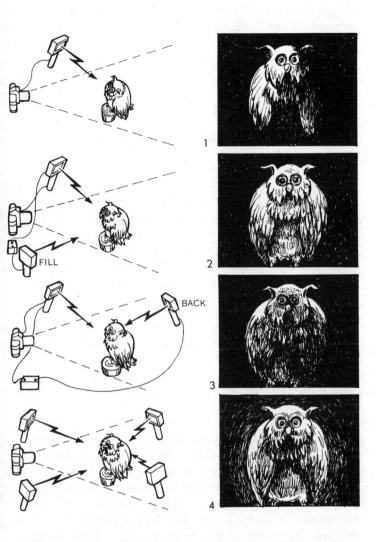

Lighting at night. **1** Only one head spotlight effect. **2** Two heads as in daylight: black background. **3** Two heads, using one as a main light and one to produce rim lighting from behind. **4** Using four heads, a moonlight effect can be produced. The backlights should be closer than front lights to give a strong rim lighting effect.

99

serious use you anticipated for trying out flash, and bulbs are certainly cheaper if only a few shots are hoped for. They give a lot of light for their size though this can be for a longer exposure time than for electronic. This is easily overcome as, often, there will be a time when the bird is still, having just alighted on a branch. With practice and luck, by making a slight noise as the bird lands, imitating a mouse perhaps, you can make it look towards the camera. The disadvantage of bulbs is that they must be changed after each shot. If the bird sees this (particularly owls) it may not return to the nest for the rest of the night. It may also attack your hand, or any part of you emerging from the hide. If you use bulbs make sure they can be easily changed from inside the hide with as little of yourself showing as possible. Electronic flash has the advantage of not having to be altered once it is set up.

A single head of flash can be used at night, as long as it is not too close to the camera and provides some modelling. Moonlight tends to provide an atmosphere of its own, very different from daylight. A flash head behind the bird gives a backlit highlight with another head to give some detail on the front of the subject, and imparts a moonlit effect to a photograph.

A similar set up to that of daylight can be used by turning round the two lights on the background, so that they light the subject from behind.

Open flash

This is a term used for leaving the shutter of the camera open and then just firing the flash to make an exposure. Naturally, this has to be done in near-dark conditions as otherwise the film will be very quickly fogged. Working with sensitive animals in the dark this method eliminates any noise from the camera. Unless the night is very black parts of the surrounding subject-matter will record slightly on the film. This may be considered advantageous, but can also lead to double images or an image of the background showing through the lighter areas of the subject. If a large subject is to be photographed at night the same flash can be set off in many different positions to illuminate, say, different sections of a tree, which are going to be part of the surroundings in a

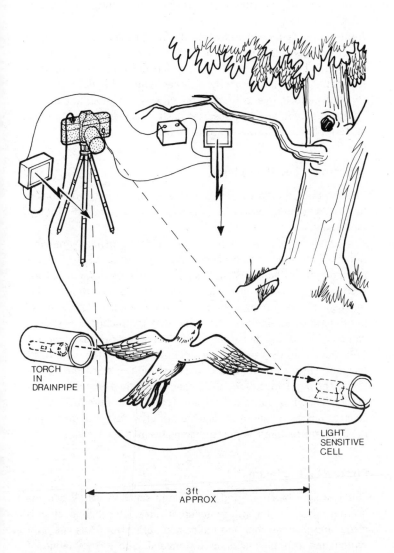

TORCH
IN
DRAINPIPE

LIGHT
SENSITIVE
CELL

3ft
APPROX

Using a simple photo-electric beam to trigger the camera. Infra-red beams are available too, and work in a similar way. Some form of mechanical shutter release is necessary, unless a power winder is used: this can then be wired up to the light sensitive cell.

photograph. If everything else remains dark this can produce exciting results.

If the shutter is opened at dusk on the aperture set for the flash, say f22, as it gets dark it may be possible to get a slight density of the sky on the film, rendering the main subject area still as a silhouette so that it becomes properly exposed when the flash is fired. Practice perfects this technique, but always remember to close the shutter after you have exposed the flash. This way you do not take all your photographs on one piece of film.

Movement and flying birds

The short duration of electronic flash enables sharp photographs to be taken where otherwise they would be blurred through movement.

The problems of small birds in the garden, constantly moving, hanging on nut baskets and swinging pieces of fat, makes photography difficult. With flash at speeds of around 1/1000 second much of this movement is stopped. As mentioned earlier the use of flash at your bird table gives you a new range of photographic possibilities. We know that computerized flashguns can be cheated into giving much shorter speeds. Speeds of around 1/10 000–1/20 000 second are sufficient to freeze the wing beats of many small birds, provided the flash unit is close enough to them. The problem is to fire the camera at the time when the bird is in the plane of focus, actually flying. Trial and error produces a low success rate as human reactions are not often fast enough to give the accuracy required. A photo-electric beam is the answer.

Photo-electric beam

This is a light beam shining onto a light sensitive cell. When the beam is broken or the light switched off, an electrical connection is made, and this can then fire the camera. Effectively, this is a light switch and can be made up by anyone with a knowledge of electrical circuits. The light source can range between a car battery and bulb, and an ordinary domestic torch.

The camera shutter release is simply a solenoid, which, when a current is passed through it, pushes a pin forward into the camera. These are available commercially though you can make your own. Even a simple mousetrap can be adapted successfully to fire a conventional cable release. There is obvious difficulty setting up this kind of arrangement, but birds flying onto perches or directly to a bird table or nest have a definite line of flight. The beam can be made to span this, and with a piece of string you can focus in the middle. Hopefully this will give you a starting point to work from. There is always a slight delay between the beam being cut and the camera and flash being fired so, depending on the speed at which the bird is flying, an allowance has to be made. The camera as in other forms of remote control, has to be wound on after each shot. The actual beam itself is invisible provided the source is covered, with a small piece of plastic drainpipe for example, and the receiving cell can also be concealed in the same way. This also helps to keep off the rain.

Infra-red beams are a more expensive though more efficient light source and can be used with the following advantages: (i) the emitter and receiver are both in the same watertight container; (ii) a reflector disc is all that is needed at the other end of the beam; (iii) a bulb flashes when it is correctly aligned.

Birds at the Nest

One of the most time-consuming activities of bird photography is the field work necessary. Nest-finding is no exception.

Looking for nests

Random searching of bushes and hedges may reveal some nests that are at a reasonable height for photographing. Some species need more concentrated efforts; establish first, that they are in fact present in the area, and then observe them from a distance through binoculars to see their activities and where they go. By camouflaging yourself you can sit unnoticed in a tree or at some other vantage point.

When looking for your own nests in this way you may come across other nests as a result. All bird photographers must be prepared to spend this time in the field, for though friendly gardeners, farmers, gamekeepers and the like may produce many more things for you to see in a much shorter time, you gain far more knowledge by looking for yourself. Observations through binoculars teaches you how birds behave normally without interference. It also tells you from which direction they fly into the nest; where they regularly land and even where they feed and catch food. All this is invaluable in helping you to assess how best to photograph birds in typical attitudes.

Positioning your hide

Bringing a hide up to working distance usually takes several days—sometimes many days, again depending very much on the bird you have chosen to photograph and the nature of its habitat, all of which must influence your approach. A bird nesting in dense woodland makes it easier to camouflage a hide than one nesting on a bare hillside.

There are two ways of getting your hide into the correct working position. One is by moving it erected across a suitably large distance over the necessary period of time. The other is to build it very slowly in front of the bird if the nature of the nesting site makes it impractical or impossible for lateral movement to take place. The latter case is applicable only for tree- and cliff-nesting species, and birds in other awkward spots. Do not be ambitious at first. Try photographing a nest in a shrub, hedge or grassy piece of land to give yourself the necessary experience of using a hide for the first time.

Time of introduction

Disturbance of a nest will almost inevitably cause failure or desertion by the parents especially if done at the wrong time. The best time to introduce a hide is after the eggs have hatched and the young are three or four days old. Before this, from when the eggs are chipping on their second day, the adults are very attentive and need to keep the young warm, so any form of disturbance must be avoided. The same is true for nest-building and egg-laying. The parents have much less attraction to an empty nest and will easily move to build another elsewhere if they are disturbed too much early on.

With species whose young walk within 24 hours of being born, a hide will have to be introduced while the eggs are still being incubated. Careful observation is therefore necessary to establish how old the eggs are and when they are likely to hatch. This is not always possible since the discovery of a completed clutch of eggs will give you no clue as to how old they are.

Discovery of a nest of large young can also be very tricky. If the young are likely to leave within a day or two, which can be ascertained from the growth of their feathers, the introduction of hide and camera may prove too much for them and they may leave early as a result. Flash can cause young to 'explode' in this fashion, if introduced too late, and once out of the nest they cannot get back in. They become easy prey especially if unable to fly, as often it is the last 24 hours in the nest which enable them to gain the power of flight. Unless daylight photography is possible from slightly further away than normal, photography in these circumstances is best forgotten.

Time of day is also very important. Moving a hide in the evening is definitely not recommended as a bird may be less likely to return to the nest once it begins to get dark.

Gardening

With many nest sites it is frequently desirable to remove some pieces of growing matter which may obscure a good view of the nest and parent birds with their young. Compositionally it can be unsatisfactory to have out-of-focus branches and leaves distracting from the subject but probably the shade, camouflage or protection that the particular branch provides, was chosen by the bird as a good nest site in the first place. The quickest and simplest solution would appear to be to cut it off. *Never* do this. Not only does it open up the nest to many potential disasters from outside, but it could easily make the birds desert. Any interference with foliage must be done with extreme care and always tied back for the purpose of photography and then gently replaced afterwards. Birds that nest in dense cover do so for a purpose and should be represented photographically as doing so. A species known to nest in long grass, shown in a photograph effectively standing in bright sunlight on a mown lawn, will be an untruthful representation. When branches etc. have to be held back with string no evidence of this must be seen in the finished result if your picture is to look natural.

Operating from the hide

The first time at a nest with all your equipment is very exciting. Everything is prepared and your helper has retreated, making just enough noise for the bird to know that danger has passed. It may return at once, or possibly not for half-an-hour; whenever it does the great temptation is to take a photograph immediately. This should be avoided at all costs as it is terribly important for the bird to settle down and carry on as normal. You have probably kept the parents off the nest for quarter-of-an-hour while you got set up, so always let a feed take place before you start doing anything at all.

Noise

The longer you leave the first shot the more confidence the bird gains, and often this pays off later. By using the camera too soon the bird can be made nervous for a long time. The first few shots, in fact, are very likely to cause alarm. Noise plays a very important part.

All birds communicate by song and their hearing is acute. Although they are familiar with all the sounds associated with their environment any unnatural noise will make them curious or frightened. Considering this, as quiet a camera shutter as possible is an advantage. Some of the smaller 35 mm SLR cameras are much quieter now than those we have become accustomed to. If flash is used as well, provided the units are not too close (further than $1\frac{1}{4}$ metres or 3 ft), they will not worry the birds. Letting the flash off without the camera soon shows if this is the case or not. Although at first camera noise is a problem, at the nest it is possible to 'train' the bird to become accustomed to it. After a dozen visits it should ignore it altogether. For particularly wary species a looped tape with the noise of the camera on it, can be introduced into the hide as you move it up. Over a few days they will soon ignore it altogether. This is useful as the volume can be turned down to start with.

Blimps made from foam rubber or any kind of material are simple to put round the camera and this helps a lot, but make sure you can wind the camera on after each shot, without having to remove the blimp each time.

If the first shot causes alarm wait until the bird is continuing as normal before winding on. This noise in itself can take the birds quite a bit of time to get used to. Nervous birds frightened of camera noise can spoil a photograph. With single lens reflex cameras the mirror has to go up out of the way before the focal plane shutter comes across and exposes the film. Many small birds hear this first action and having very quick reactions already have their wings in the air when the shutter is released. This is often especially noticeable when using electronic flash. The first day in a hide with such a bird can result in no sharp photographs while it is becoming accustomed to the strange new sound.

There is, fortunately, a simple way out when using some models of SLR cameras; i.e. the 35 mm or $2\frac{1}{4}$ in. sq. These types have a mirror lock which means that the mirror can be flipped up out of the way before the shutter is released. The first noise the bird then hears is the shutter going across and this does not result in any movement at speeds above about 1/15th second. The disadvantage of this is that the position the bird will be in has to be known beforehand, as once the mirror is up vision through the viewfinder is lost. If the bird is using a perch this is easy. If not, it is possible to view the bird and then flip up the mirror while it is in the viewfinder, pause for it to react and then release the shutter.

Once the bird is used to the camera it can become more tolerant of other noises as its confidence increases. The birds may even become totally trusting which makes photography that much more exciting and rewarding.

Night-time

Daytime photography is influenced a great deal by sight and also by sound. There is always noise; birds singing and distant sounds, and one becomes much more aware of this because of the limitation of sight that the hide imposes on you. There is nearly always some noise, be it a call or a wing beat, when a bird returns to its nest in the day, and this is helpful. Very few are completely silent. Not so at night. It is, perhaps, the silence more than the loss of light that makes nocturnal photography so different from that of the day. Not only is everything quiet, but there is almost no noise from night birds as they come and go from their nests. It is only their large hungry young that give away owls and others. With an owl, though, you would be lucky to hear the rasp of its claws as it alights momentarily in its nesting hole before disappearing inside. Because you cannot see does not mean that your subject cannot see you. Being nocturnal they always can, so all your care and exactitude is just as important at night. You must be even quieter than in the day for any noise on a still night travels far. Some owls attack when they are disturbed, so wear a crash helmet and visor for safety, when hide-building and entering and leaving it. Build your hide for night photography during the day, and over the same period of time.

Most birds accept a dark red light shining at their nest site if it does not flicker. By using a heavy duty battery that will not run down over a night, you can focus and see when the bird arrives. On a bright moonlit night you can see the bird coming without the aid of a light, but you cannot always focus. With a nest with a single entrance focus in daylight and leave it set. This can provide good results.

Flash is the only successful way to photograph owls, and in some instances bulbs can be used to advantage. Owls visit their nests less often than day birds so there are long gaps during which bulbs can be changed. If this is the only kind of photography for which you envisage using flash, bulbs are the answer, being cheaper. They give out as much, if not more, light than an equivalent electronic unit, so you can light a large area round a nest site with one or two flash bulbs. An owl usually pauses for a second or two when reaching the nest, and with practice it is possible to capture this precise moment. Invariably the bird is looking away from the camera, so a slight hiss from you may cause it to look at the lens. The sound might also stop it from disappearing into a tree. If you do this be sure that the flash head is away from the camera as a flash directly into the owl's eyes can upset it.

Make certain you always change the bulbs from inside the hide, and also that the bird has left the area. Sometimes the bulb can be changed while the bird is still in the nest out of your sight, though there is always the risk that it or another adult, is sitting nearby. A hand appearing suddenly from the hide could provoke an attack. It is clear therefore, that although there are pecuniary advantages in using bulbs, electronic flash is probably safer.

Birds in Action

Action photographs of birds often say far more about them than those taken in a more placid pose. It is frequently desirable to show birds using their wings but the technical problems, possibly only solved with flash, make this difficult especially with small, fast flying birds.

General approach

The fundamental problem is twofold. First, you must be in the right place with your camera to capture whatever action is going on. Second, you must be near enough to that action to obtain a reasonably-sized image in the viewfinder. Undoubtedly luck plays a great part, and the more time spent in the field the more chance opportunities present themselves.

Action can be anticipated but you may have to wait a long time. Opportunities appear in two ways—unexpectedly, and from a calculated piece of fieldwork that you know should give you the observed result.

The first requires quick reactions, good anticipation and complete familiarity with your equipment. This last point is extremely important, more so than any other branch of bird photography as any operative mistake means that you have lost the chance of the photograph and will rarely get another try. Sudden action might occur while you are busy with something in the hide, or even while you are out walking or stalking.

The second approach is to get close to the subject while it is engaged in a piece of familiar action. Each season you amass information while nest-finding or generally bird-watching. So it is always worthwhile to keep a notebook for recording interesting pieces of behaviour that you might wish to photograph some day.

If a bird is known to like dust bathing, eating ants or is particularly aggressive during courtship or when it has young, it may be worth trying to capture this particular behaviour. It may happen only once or twice over a relatively short space of time which is very restricting. Before going to all the trouble of building a hide and possibly getting no result, it is better to attempt something more predictable; colonial birds for example, or large birds in flight which can give you a good start in this challenging branch of bird photography.

Clothing

The right clothing can make all the difference. Incorrect wear can actually prevent you obtaining any result at all. Remember the needs of your subject as well as your own requirements; wear natural fibres (wool, cotton) rather than synthetics which, when rubbed together, make a noise causing possible stress to the bird.
All clothing should be functional and of good camouflage, but this still leaves hands and face exposed, and these can be seen from a long way off. A coloured gauze face mask with eye-holes works well in winter, though it can become hot and irritating in summer. Mittens keep your hands warm while leaving your fingers free to operate the camera.

Cameras

More than with other forms of bird photography it is essential to be viewing the subject exactly as the camera sees it, when so many other variables are at stake. All SLR cameras give you this freedom. For anything on the move it is necessary to have a fast shutter speed setting on the camera body. On some of the more expensive cameras 1/2000 second is the fastest, though for most situations 1/1000 or 1/500 second is perfectly adequate, and possible with most makes.
Fully automatic cameras are also available where by setting the film speed on them, a correct exposure is calculated, and the aperture or shutter speed is mechanically changed to guarantee the result. For action this is a great help; you do not have to worry about the exposure and are able to concentrate solely on the

subject. In good light this gives considerable freedom. These cameras work by setting either the shutter speed or the aperture and the camera then adjusts the other. If the aperture is set the speed will alter according to the light available and you can end up with too slow a speed causing the subject to be a blur. Alternatively, by setting the speed the aperture is adjusted. In low light it may be that the aperture is unable to go wide enough for the set speed thereby preventing a photograph from being taken. This is a disadvantage especially with the chance of photographing something unusual. It is far better to have some kind of result even if it shows technical shortcomings.

A through the lens meter gives good results with practice. As a rule the highlight areas if large, as with skies, tend to overrule the reading, exposing a sky correctly and leaving the less bright subject much darker. Experience of pointing the camera towards the ground and reading off a similarly bright object as the subject, will give more satisfactory results. Quick checks of the light throughout the day will enable you to keep the camera at a setting ready for action. However, if you rely on this form of metering or choose an automatic camera, always be sure to carry spare batteries; they are only small but can save the day.

If the camera does not have a built in meter then a separate hand meter serves very well. It can slip into a pocket and is easily carried. It can present a problem when wanting to photograph quickly; a reading beforehand, one with the sun out and one in (cloud) shadow can often be taken at the start of an expedition and will then act as a good guide for most of a day, at least until the sun goes in or it starts to rain.

Motor driven cameras

In a fast moving event like a bird flying or taking off, the amount of different photographs that you can take is restricted by the number of times you can wind the film on. Winding on takes time and usually results in the camera having to be moved away from the eye to let you do so. You might lose the image and you certainly will lose the plane of focus.

An automatic wind-on overcomes these problems. On pressing the

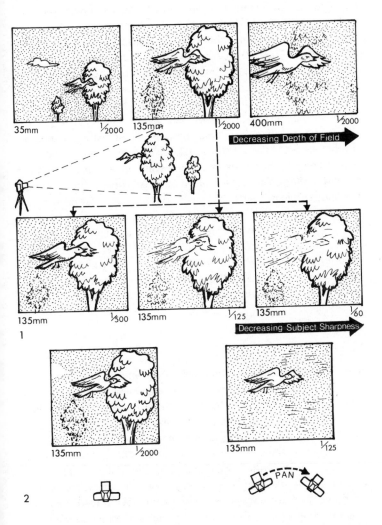

1 With a camera in a fixed position, the diagrams show the effect of different lenses and different shutter speeds. **2** Two ways of overcoming subject movement; with a high shutter speed or by panning with the subject, which causes the background to become a blur. The latter isolates the subject much better than the former.

shutter release the film winds on automatically immediately after, enabling you to maintain vision through the viewfinder and pan and focus without losing the subject.

Power winders or 'autowinders' are available for many makes of SLR cameras. They are an expensive extra and only worth buying if you are going to attempt a lot of flight photography. They can also be used successfully with remote control as they eliminate the otherwise necessary disturbance of winding the film on manually. The specifications of power winders vary according to the make and model, but there is a choice between single frame winding on (each time after the shutter is released it winds on to the next frame) and continuous exposure and wind on, at three frames per second or more. This continuous motion is achieved for as long as the shutter release remains depressed. The more advanced motor drives can also wind the film back into the cassette when it comes to the end, and can run off rechargeable or penlight batteries, the former adding considerably to the initial cost, and the latter being used up quickly in the field. So, always have plenty of spares.

You will often find yourself out in the open, carrying your camera ready for any eventuality, so both you and your equipment need to be mobile.

Lenses

In more predictable situations shorter focal length like 135 mm, can be used to capture the sudden burst of activity which may occur at a bird table for example, when you are set up to it. Similarly, at a hide, if something happens at nest while you are photographing there you will be ready to record the unexpected.

Most action requires a longer focal length lens as the subject is often that much further away, and probably difficult to approach any closer. A disadvantage of long lenses is that their widest apertures may not always be wide enough. With a 400 mm f3.5 lens the choice may be between one with a maximum aperture of f3.5 and another of f5.6. The wider aperture (f3.5) lets in more light, and therefore can be used with a faster shutter speed (ideal for action) in equivalent conditions. But the larger aperture makes the lens bulkier, heavier and, invariably, more expensive.

Optical performance at full aperture is not usually very good except with the dearer makes, but improves with stopping down to a smaller aperture. A lens used stopped down to f11 or f16 gives a sharper photograph than if used at its fullest aperture.

Most expensive lenses are optically superior, but good results at full aperture can be obtained from relatively inexpensive equipment.

A 400 mm–500 mm lens is the longest focal length of lens that is practicable for hand-held work but even then some means of support is useful. A 135 mm may be all that is needed, for some birds, when flying, are much bigger with their wings extended than when they are standing. Although you may get a smaller image then with a longer lens, you have much greater depth of field at your disposal for the same aperture on a longer focal length lens. This makes a big difference in practice—particularly to start with.

Automatic and manual lenses

Automatic lenses let you view the subject with the diaphragm fully open, but as soon as the shutter is released they automatically stop down to the selected aperture.

With manual lenses, you either have to view the subject with the lens ready stopped down, which can make focusing difficult as you get a darker image. Or you view with the aperture wide open and then stop down to shoot. This is not practical when working with any sort of action as you either forget to do it, or, in the rush, stop down by the wrong amount. Manual lenses are cheaper to buy and are as good optically as automatic types of the same make.

Automatic lenses give you the freedom of clear focusing and correct aperture control without any worry. There often is no time to stop down at the vital moment.

Film stock

Fast film speeds in colour make all the difference to action photography; 200 ASA film gives plenty of scope and good colour. This branch of photography is where the higher speed films come into their own, as they allow the welcome combination of a small aperture and reasonably high shutter speed. This means that you can achieve a sharp photograph in many conditions because there is sufficient depth of field to cover sudden movement as well as a fast enough shutter speed to 'freeze' the subject.

In black and white photography, 400 ASA film is ideal and can be carefully processed to give quite a fine grain print.

In certain circumstances film may be updated to give twice or more its recommended speed. In colour this sometimes tends to break the colour rendering down and increase the grain size though forced, or 'pushed' processing to double the effective film speed from 200 to 400 ASA is naturally very successful. Most processing laboratories will do this for you. Forced processing of black and white film also, increases grain size. But by this means you may increase the effective speed by up to 2 stops (four times the ASA speed rating) with success.

Shutter speeds

The longer the focal length of the lens the greater the magnification, and the more that camera movement shows up relative to the subject. This, of course, leads to unsharp photographs. The faster the shutter speed you use the more likely it is that you will get a sharp image. To be able to use the top speeds on your camera conditions usually have to be fairly bright even when using a fast film. Even so, this is not always the best approach as sometimes it can detract from the finished result. A picture of a bird flying against trees with the trees as frozen-looking as the bird produces an unnatural effect. This is often produced by using *too* fast a shutter speed, the subject becoming lost in the background.

By panning the camera with a flying bird the background appears to move across the viewfinder at great speed. By keeping the bird in approximately the same position in the frame it becomes an advantage to use a slower shutter speed as that causes the background to become blurred behind the sharply-rendered subject. This gives a good impression of movement and can be used to great effect. It largely depends on the subject as to what shutter speeds work best, but with the larger gliding birds, speeds of 1/125 second can produce good results even with a 400 mm lens. Even slower shutter speeds may be used effectively with your camera on a tripod or well supported. Try photographing a group of birds sitting or standing, at varying shutter speeds of 1/60 second, 1/30 second, 1/15 second or less. By taking several shots you may eventually get a few frames in which one or two of the birds have not moved during the exposure, with the remainder showing varying amounts of movement, creating a realistic atmosphere of activity. Wing patterns, although not sharp, can produce attractive designs and some photographs convey an interesting impression of flight.

The correct shutter speed for birds in action may differ between subjects, especially if there is some advantage in showing movement connected with the bird itself, like flapping wings. With gliding birds which are not flapping their wings, 1/125 second is sufficient if panning with a 135 mm lens and, possibly, with practice, a 400 mm lens. For anything moving faster, 1/250 second and 1/500 second should be used, though wingtips may well remain blurred as even 1/1000 second cannot arrest this rapid movement. The closer the moving subject is to the camera, then the faster you have to move the camera to keep up with it, and therefore the faster shutter speeds are necessary.

It is almost impossible to show most of the smaller birds in flight except by high speed flashlight because of the difficulty of getting close to them in the wild and the rapidity of their wingbeats.

Supports

Photography of moving, particularly flying, birds is certainly more conveniently achieved without a tripod. Tripods are the best form of support but are cumbersome to carry and on many of them there is no tilt head to allow vertical movement. This cuts out their use on birds flying immediately overhead.

The next best tool to a tripod might be a monopod. These resemble one telescopic leg from a tripod with a camera bush and ball and socket head on the top. They prevent any movement in one plane altogether which is useful.

Another good general purpose support is the rifle grip. This can be handmade from the wooden butt of a rifle, and is ideal for an SLR used with, perhaps, a 300 mm–500 mm lens. Commercially-made metal shoulder pods are available and work the same way; by pressing the 'butt' end into your shoulder stability is gained and you can swing comfortably onto the subject. A trigger as in a gun fires the camera by means of the built-in cable release. A rifle grip may be used anywhere, and in a standing, sitting or lying down position.

With a lot of practice it is possible to hand-hold a 400 mm for flying birds so do not feel that shoulder supports are essential. Always make use of available cover and support; use the ground if at all possible and when firing the shutter concentrate all the time on keeping the lens steady. Some people always hold their breath just before firing but others will not as they maintain that heartbeats jog the lens anyway.

With any photograph firing the shutter and losing the image due to the rising mirror is not the end of the exposure but the beginning. So with movement always follow the image through, keep your eye firmly to the viewfinder until after the mirror has returned. This is the nearest you will get to seeing the actual image you took until the film is processed. Many photographs, especially of moving subjects, can be spoilt by stopping the panning movement too soon. By keeping the image in the viewfinder before and after exposure you have the chance to check that it has not moved its position in the frame during the exposure.

Colonial seabirds

Seabirds present such a wide variety of opportunities for the photographer that anyone wishing to attempt any form of action could not do better than to start with this type of subject. Even in the winter flocks of gulls make excellent subjects for quickening your reactions and trying out equipment and techniques. Colonial breeders are as prone as other birds to disturbance but there are a number of places where limited access gives plenty of scope, and often the birds are used to seeing humans which makes them more trusting and easier to approach. Nevertheless you still have to be very cautious. The season when the adults have hungry young is the best time to go. This way there is no danger of keeping a nervous bird off chilling eggs which might die, and there should be plenty of visits by parents eager to feed their young.

The biggest temptation photographically is to attempt too much. The whole atmosphere, the number of birds, the noise and the smell are all very strong factors influencing you and affecting your concentration. The first few times it is a very exciting experience. After even half-an-hour of following birds round in the viewfinder and trying to photograph as many as possible, not only will you have a headache, but you will probably have run out of all your film so take plenty. It is much better to concentrate on one particular bird at a time. More photographs will be successful if you adopt this discipline.

Ground-nesting seabirds will accept people in close proximity to their nests without a hide, but only if you make slow progress towards them. This is much better done 'on all fours' than by walking up to them, which will cause them distress. By crouching down by a rock the birds will usually come to accept your presence and, with luck, will carry on normally.

In such conditions you need to have all your equipment as mobile and compact as possible. Do not be so cluttered with it that you cannot move very far when you come to take your photographs. Before setting out make a list of everything you might need; different lengths of lens are always worth carrying though sometimes a zoom lens is the only answer. A 400 mm, 135 mm and 35 mm is a useful all-round selection. The 400 mm is for selective flight shots; the 135 mm can be used for flying birds as many will come close—this is ideal too, for individual birds on rocks or at their nests. Extension tubes might also be useful. Distant parts of the colony can be shot with this lens. The 35 mm wide angle is good for showing the whole habitat. Try and get an interesting foreground as a large depth of field with this lens gives a sharp picture throughout. By the sea have UV or haze-reducing filters on all the lenses, not only to improve the image quality but to protect them from spray. To remove moisture, use a clean chamois leather or absorbent lens tissue.

Finding the best exposure for seabirds is difficult due to their white plumage. In sunlight a very high reading is often obtained. With colour materials this reading must be used if the feather detail of the bird is required. If more exposure is given the white plumage will 'bleach out' and appear generally overexposed. With such a bird against a deep blue sea, the actual exposure difference may be too great for the colour film to be able to cope with. This being the case, the sea would then be rendered darker than was accurate, so it is much better to photograph in more subdued light conditions. A light covering of cloud over the sun gives a much more even lighting over the subject and far less contrast.

Birds flying overhead in bright sunlight may have the sun shining through their feathers making them look almost transparent. Exposure here is tricky; do not take a reading from the sky as it will be too bright and make the underside of the bird look black in the finished result. Expose for a soft shadow reading taken from something of similar tone around you. You can then record shadow detail in the underside of the bird and produce a highlight of the feathers which are catching the sun. With black and white it is not difficult to obtain satisfactory results in full sunlight.

Purposely overexposing the subject and then under developing the negative reduces contrast so by rating a film that is normally ASA 125, at ASA 64, you can give the subject a stop more exposure. By reducing the development time by about 20 per cent, a negative is produced with detail in shadow and highlight areas. The film can be rated at still lower speed and further experimentation will tell what produces the best results for you. Too much under-rating however, can make the film, in effect, too slow to be of much use. A useful working distance of 7 ft can be achieved with a 135 mm lens though be careful not to sit on the flight line of the bird to the nest as this can cause distress. Observation beforehand soon shows from which direction the bird flies. Once you have finished taking your photographs retreat with as much caution as you used in approaching. To stand up suddenly can easily frighten the bird and, if it is near cliffs, may send young not able to fly properly tumbling to their deaths. Cliffs are very dangerous places though they are good for flight shots of birds gliding and hovering on the updraught of wind coming up the sheer face.

When working anywhere with large numbers of birds in close proximity, there is often much interaction between them, not always apparent at first. By watching one individual it can be seen that there is no easy path to take from the sea back to its nest when carrying food, as so many others try to take it for themselves. Panning round with your camera and following the flight of such a bird is great fun, but it is virtually impossible to keep it in focus all the time. One of the best-tried methods is to prefocus at a predetermined distance and wait for the bird to fly into focus. A certain amount of anticipation and judgement is called for to press the shutter at the right moment. If you are shooting a sequence with a motordrive you have to keep re-focusing on the bird all the time. This works best if the subject is flying across the field of view. With a bird flying straight towards or away from you the focus changes so quickly that the pre-focus method is probably the best.

Many seabirds breed on islands and the only way over is by boat. Moving on the water like this does not make a good platform for photography because of the constant wave motion and vibration of the engine. On calmer days there is scope for shots of birds taking off from the water and skimming over it, but because of the additional movements the fastest shutter speeds need to be used to ensure sharpness.

Stalking

Stalking a bird with a camera is exhilarating and a great challenge; camouflage, caution and quietness are the main factors to worry about, operation of your camera must be second nature.

Birds are always on the alert so they will almost certainly fly away if you walk straight up to them. If a bird is engaged in some definite activity such as feeding or singing there is more chance of getting close to it without being seen. Often the best way is by crawling on your stomach, especially in open ground where any upright is immediately noticed. Make yourself as flat as possible and choose a route to your potential subject, which has some natural features for you to hide behind and look round (*not* over) to see if the subject is still unaware of you.

Push the camera in front of you together with your binoculars. Black or camouflage tape can be put over any shiny parts of the camera or lens to stop the sun catching it and giving your presence away. With extreme caution you might get to within 20 or 30 ft. If the bird sees you, freeze, and do not move at all for some time; it may accept you and continue feeding. The camera being in front of you makes it easier in the latter stages to edge forward with it to your eye, so that you can get at least one shot even if the subject does see you.

After stalking for some time you will probably be out of breath so your heart beats faster, making it difficult to hold the camera still. Up-ended binoculars make a good little support for the camera lens and help to steady the camera for an exposure. Another result of an energetic stalk is that your breath can steam up the viewfinder. The only way to prevent this is to blow out of the sides of your mouth and hold your breath when viewing and taking the photograph. Because there is less light in areas of denser cover a tripod can be used. Again, by moving slowly between trees and bushes, you can edge it in front of you. A wooden model will not catch the sun nor make a noise. Although it helps you to cope with slower shutter speeds a tripod can sometimes be an encumbrance, and you may find it easier to use branches as supports.

Action from hides

When working from a hide something spectacular can happen close at hand or some distance away. To deal with this situation have a wide enough opening in the front of your hide for a long lens which can then be panned from side to side. You must still have a net for the lens to go through and, for fear of giving yourself away, may not be able to pan as quickly as when working without a hide.

When an unexpected bird does appear in front of the hide the temptation is to move the camera straight on to it. You might get one shot, though there is an equal chance that as soon as it arrives it will be taking in its surrounds and looking at the lens. If this should suddenly move the bird will certainly be frighted and fly off. If you can, always wait until it walks into the frame, and once it has done so you can then pan with it which it should hardly notice.

With flash used at the nest most action is frozen, particularly the restless movement of the young when a parent arrives with food. Many photographs taken with available light, especially some early bird photographs, nearly always show the young as a blurred mass, as the long shutter speeds caught the parent motionless, but never the offspring. Any wing movements at the nest can also be arrested with flash which, although on occasions produces an unnaturally-lit result, does give a lot of information about the young.

Available light

The amount of natural light on the subject can easily be determined by the use of a light meter or, if you have one built into your camera, this will give you a similar result. Suffice it to say you have no control over this though you should always try to select a location with as much light on it as possible.

Captive Birds

Any involvement with photographing birds is inevitably going to cause them some kind of disturbance and stress. Consequently it is very important to decide how much disturbance or stress you are prepared to inflict on a bird to obtain a good photograph. Anyone having an affinity with their subject will always put the welfare of the bird as their first priority, being ready to abandon photography at any stage. Refusal of a bird to return to the nest is an obvious indication. This must be the only reasonable attitude.

Ethics

Captive birds pose another problem and may make ostensibly easier subjects to photograph. With a little skill they can be made to look wild and free, but it is surely unethical to try and pass them off as such. Subjects taken in this way must always be clearly labelled as being captive and/or controlled. There is now great interest in aviculture and zoos, wildlife parks and aviaries all provide plenty of scope for this branch of photography. To want to photograph such species you must be motivated by a different force from that of wanting to photograph them in the wild.

Catching birds yourself and putting them into a controlled environment might, then, seem by far the easiest way to obtain good pictures. Indiscriminate bird catching is certainly *not* recommended. Training is necessary for handling captive birds, and it is illegal in Britain to catch them without a licence, so make sure the law is observed. Although you can get technically satisfactory results there is no sense of achievement in doing so, and in most such cases the birds are very frightened and look so. There is little chance of any natural behaviour in unnatural surroundings.

Captive birds have a place in bird photography for scientific purposes and in situations where they may be very rare or new to science. It can be the only way to get sufficient close-up detail of an eye, beak or plumage, where in the wild it would be impossible to get near enough.

As the photographer you must decide *why* you wish to use a totally controlled species and *how* you will use it. Never try to pass it off as something it is not. Unfortunately it has been done, not only with healthy birds but with sick ones and stuffed ones too. To indulge in this only brings the whole of genuine photography into disrepute. Picture editors may occasionally be taken in, but any naturalist or experienced photographer can easily recognize a fake photograph of this kind.

The moral obligation to reflect on your own actions is always present. If you have any doubts about a course of action play safe and do not do it. Many nests need 'gardening' before they can be photographed (Ch. 6) but do not ever cut away any of the branches obstructing your view. The bird has chosen this cover specially, and by removing it you leave the bird and its young exposed to predators, and the harsh effects of the weather. Tie back the foliage if necessary, and then the nest site can be arranged exactly as it was after photography is over.

Using a mirror (Ch. 3) as an aid to display photography may upset the bird more than is apparent so never leave one out for too long. A potential mate could be ignored and possibly lost, though there is no strong evidence for this.

Indiscriminate baiting of birds in the breeding season should always be avoided. At this time there is no shortage of natural food, and the unnatural food (e.g. bread) put out by you could well be taken for the young which might die as a result, being unable to digest it. Carrion put down near nesting birds will endanger their nests from the attracted carrion eaters.

Zoos and caged birds

A day at the zoo studying birds can be great fun. The chance of seeing so many different species in close detail can never be achieved in the wild in so short a space of time, and there is seldom the opportunity to observe at such close quarters. In most cases photography is difficult as the subjects are completely enclosed. The cages often have wire fronts and sides, or glass too. Some species are kept indoors so flash has to be used.

Many birds could be in bad condition, looking scruffy with feathers missing. They all moult at one time or another which can be clearly observed in a zoo, and often accounts for the bird's unhealthy appearance. In the wild you do not come across this so much, as many birds are photographed during the breeding season when they are in peak condition. By the end of this time they can look very tatty, feeding the last of their second, or even third, broods. As a result of these problems it may be virtually impossible to hide the fact that these birds are caged, so the best solution is to show the situation for what it is, cage and all. There are ways round many of these difficulties to get pleasant close-ups of particular species which would not be possible any other way. Wire cages are the popular form of enclosing birds and taking photographs from normal viewing positions always includes a predominance of wire which spoils the result. By placing the lens right up against the wire it is possible to reduce its effect almost completely. This reduction depends on the mesh size and precise position of the camera on the wire, and the focal length of lens and the aperture used.

With a very small mesh size pressed in front of the lens the effect produced is one of a very hazy image—almost like an extreme soft focus screen. As the mesh size increases there are bigger gaps and less wire to break up the image. Place the camera as close to the wire as possible making sure you do not get a cross of wire in the centre of the lens.

If too short a focal length lens is used, because of its large depth of field the foreground wire is seen in sharper focus. A longer focal length lens therefore has the effect of isolating the subject from the foreground and background because of the relatively much shallower depth of field. Birds of many sizes can occur in different cages so that no one lens will serve for every purpose. A 90 mm and 135 mm are probably the most useful focal lengths for 'portraits'. A lens of greater or shorter focal length can also come in handy, so this is possibly an occasion to use a really good zoom to cover these variations.

Aperture control is important here too as, if made too small, it will give too much depth of field and bring the wire into prominence. With automatic lenses it is only too easy to forget to stop down with the preview button and check to see what effect your chosen f stop has on the scene. Most cameras have this feature, so always use it in this type of situation.

Knowing where to focus is always a problem; stopping down a lens brings more into focus behind the subject than in front of it. With the preview button you can see how much.

Not only are foregrounds a nuisance, but so also are backgrounds. A longer focal length lens might throw this sufficiently out of focus, but often it may be better to find another cage where there are perches and foliage, or a place with the background too far away to matter. If you have to record a species in this way make sure that you have the correct foliage showing with the particular species of bird. An Australian bird photographed in an American bush will take in some people, but not all.

Open enclosures

Many species such as waterfowl, flamingoes, cranes etc., are displayed in open enclosures where you have only to look over a wire fence to take photographs. Some, like macaws or parakeets, might even be free-flying which gives a marvellous opportunity for flight photography against the sky. Many more in larger cages can fly from one perch to another. This gives more scope than the smaller wire cages.

A tripod can be really useful at a zoo especially in the large enclosures. It enables you to use longer lens like the 400 mm which can totally isolate a subject. It also lets you select your subject and leave the camera focused on it until it starts behaving in a way you wish to record. And as many of the birds are in such close proximity the tripod's additional weight is not so much of a hinderance as on long treks over wild country.

Many occasions arise when a good specimen is found in perfect surroundings, but it is asleep! Although photographs of this nature are interesting and difficult to get except in a zoo, you may often want a photograph showing as many useful points about a bird as possible. When it wakes up, for instance, it might yawn or stretch its wing or start preening, all of these activities make interesting photographs and may be well worth waiting for. For some subjects you may have to wait a long time. Making a sudden noise will attract the attention of wild birds fairly quickly but in a zoo this tactic does not always work as the birds become used to people and all the noise associated with them.

Large enclosures give you more chance, especially with water birds, some of which may fly round, landing, taking off, fighting at feeding time etc., all giving many opportunities of action. Backgrounds must be watched carefully as many can make a bird look quite out of place. With flying birds, buildings which you did not notice, can easily appear in the finished result. Waterbirds often have their wings clipped to prevent them from flying and this may be done to other species. It involves the removal of the primary feathers from one of the wings and this can always be seen even when the bird is sitting or swimming. When looking for detail in a photograph they are conspicuous by their absence. Many photographs of waterfowl like this are published by unaware editors, or because no suitable pictures of sufficient detail have been taken in the wild.

The more creative photographer can make pictures from the many colours and shapes to be found everywhere in zoos. Flamingoes, when sleeping, completely submerge their heads and graceful necks in their plumage which makes an interesting sight. Such photographs can be taken with available light as they all occur outdoors. Many zoos have to keep much of the aviculture inside for warmth. Although a lot of these bird houses have large glass roofs to let in as much daylight as possible it is seldom enough to use as a light source. To make things worse, many subjects are behind glass which, although it eliminates any problems with wire, creates another—reflections.

Flash

Flash is the only answer indoors but reflections from a glass surface can be a problem. The following points are worth bearing in mind.

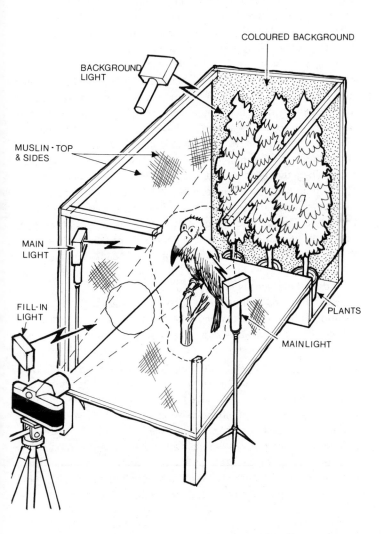

COLOURED BACKGROUND

BACKGROUND LIGHT

MUSLIN · TOP & SIDES

MAIN LIGHT

FILL-IN LIGHT

PLANTS

MAINLIGHT

A bird studio for captive portraits. Muslin sides and top are very important for ventilation and to prevent the bird from hurting itself if it flies off the perch. Try not to have the bird too near the background.

129

Always try to get the camera as close to the glass as you can. This will eliminate reflections of the camera body and from other lights. The body can be taped to cover the shiny parts, or a large sheet of black card can be used with a hole cut out for the lens only. Be sure the glass is as clean as possible. You can only clean the outside, of course!

Position the flash away from the camera axis. Two heads are better than one for this. The main light can be placed as close to the glass as possible so no reflections are caused. The second flash may have to be further away so be very careful about the angle at which you position it. A small lamp is handy to have with you as, shone from the position of either flash unit, it will immediately show where the reflection will appear. One flash head can be just as effective on some small birds especially if they are next to a white wall which, with the light bounced off it, can act as a useful fill in. Using two flash units, or heads, and a camera is impossible on your own without either an assistant or some kind of adjustable support that fits onto the camera to support the flash heads. You may need to improvise with this. Perforated metal for the arms or an amended angle lamp attached to a metal bar that screws into the camera produces a unit which can be picked up in one hand leaving the other free to focus. If the lamps are too near equal power, the fill in can be diffused with acetate material or a handkerchief placed over the front. A few tests beforehand soon tell you what result to expect. Not only does a handkerchief cut down the amount of light but it also diffuses it, giving a much softer and more pleasing result. If you have to photograph through wire with the flash some way off, shadows from the wire may show on the subject, so alway have it close if possible.

Before anything of this nature is attempted, permission must first be obtained from the zoo authorities. Some zoos have strict controls over photography, especially when using flash. Some practical help from one of the staff could save a lot of time.

Portable studios

Having decided that you want to photograph birds in captivity the surest way to get a very technical photograph showing all the details you wish, is to make some kind of enclosure or large box which is ideally suited for photography. The design should include a suitable perch for the bird to sit on and a background. The perch ideally should be changed for each new species as many different species all sitting on the same perch will look rather unimaginative. Ideally backgrounds should be changed as well. Simple pieces of card will do in acceptable colours like blues and greens, and these can be hand-painted as a blurred sky or woodland scene. You might want to design the 'studios' to take pot plants at the back to give the feel of real greenery. The perch should be as far away as possible from the background to make it as out of focus as you can and also to prevent any shadows falling on it from the subject. With such an arrangement you can make use of daylight, if you make a suitable translucent roof, but flashlight is really more satisfactory. Working close to the bird a small aperture is necessary to get everything sharp, and with daylight this would mean a long exposure. Flash eliminates this. The box can be made to house all the lighting you might need and the exact design to suit your purpose can be improved at a later date. Basically, three lights are probably the minimum as one (ideally two) is needed to illuminate the background and the other two to illuminate the bird in the same way as you would light a nest site. Photographs taken like this can look too good to be true and usually appear overlit. Pointing the lamps at different angles can greatly improve some subjects by preventing this. Tropical species live in jungles constantly in shade or dappled light. Lighting them brilliantly as if they are in the open is misleading. However, if the photographs are being taken for scientific records, which justifies this kind of photography, it does not matter so much if they look unnatural. Nor is it disastrous if the birds look startled. Almost invariably birds look wary and uneasy when they are suddenly put into new environments. Those who have watched species in the field know their behaviour patterns and what is normal. One can often get a photograph of a bird in a very nervous stance and be unaware of it oneself. To overcome this allow the subject to become accustomed to its surroundings and to your presence before you attempt photography. Great patience is required for all bird photography, and this is also true in the zoo.

Confining birds in this way puts great strain on them, so work as quickly and efficiently as you can in order not to cause more stress to the bird than absolutely necessary.

Birds for this kind of photography inevitably have to be handled. It is illegal to catch birds without a licence in Britain, so only through sympathetic zoos and acquaintances will you really be able to try this studio approach. For many birds however, this could be the only way of showing them as, in certain countries, catching birds on expedition for identification is probably the only way to see them at all. Whatever you photograph, be it in a zoo or in a jungle, make careful notes on its correct identification. After going to great lengths to get the photographs it looks unconvincing if you do not know what your subject is finally.

Seasons and Weather

The weather greatly influences all our actions, especially during winter when we have the choice between going out into the cold or staying indoors where it is warm. It influences what we wear and where we go. This is particularly true for the photographer for, invariably, one puts off taking pictures unless the sun is shining. Each season brings a variety of changes in both plant growth and the weather so that your environment which is also your studio, is always different. This produces great possibilities for photography, but some of them are fleeting.

Winter

When conditions are probably hardest is the best time to start bird photography as you can have a lot of birds around with less danger of frightening them. Autumn with its brilliant colours seems to be in a constant state of change and gives you a wonderful selection of backgrounds for birds. With the colder weather frosts appear and birds in these conditions make appealing pictures, even though you yourself may get very cold out in your hide! At this time of year photographs are well worth the time they often take to obtain. A robin in the snow is a pretty sight especially when it fluffs out its feathers to let in an air gap to keep warm.

The cold can be troublesome for your equipment if, for instance, you take it from a warm house into the freezing atmosphere outside. Condensation forms on the lens and eyepiece until they cool to the new surrounding temperature. Again, once the camera has attained this temperature warm breath accumulating in a hide onto the eyepiece causes misting up and loss of image. Avoid breathing directly on to the metallic parts and the risk is reduced. To stop moisture getting on the back element of the lens it should be put outside the hide. Once on the camera it can be put in place quickly with the front element positioned outside the hide, which

133

will prevent it from being affected by body heat from inside. Only the eyepiece will mist up and can be easily cleaned with a chamois leather. I sometimes leave the camera out in the car or in the garden all day so it remains focused and at a constant temperature. But, by doing so, the battery (if you have an electronic shutter) becomes very cold and may refuse to function. So I have a spare being kept warm in my pocket.

With prolonged use in very cold conditions the lubricants in a camera may give shutter trouble. Although expensive it is possible to have your camera 'winterized' with different lubricants which work best at temperatures below freezing. Manufacturers supply this on enquiry. When you return to a warmer climate the camera will have to be 'dewinterized' to be restored to its previous working condition. Before doing any photography in difficult conditions always have your camera checked to be sure that at least you start off with it in first class condition.

When working in the cold keep the camera warm by having it as close to your body as possible. It will be kept from wind and cold if you hang it round your neck under a thick coat. Metal conducts the cold easily and at temperatures of $-20°C$ and below you can even lose some of your eyelashes against a frozen viewfinder when looking through it. Wear gloves or, preferably, mittens as very cold metal can damage the skin of your hands.

If the camera gets too cold so will the film and though it may work (it will if it has been winterized of course) it will become so brittle that it can easily snap if wound on too quickly. Therefore wind on very slowly. If the film does snap, you will have to use a changing bag to continue taking photographs. Changing bags are especially useful in windy conditions when snow can blow into the back of the camera. Care must be taken when warm hands touch a film in a changing bag as condensation soon forms whenever the temperature changes. In sub-zero conditions moisture soon freezes on the camera or the lens. This causes permanent patterns on the film emulsion. Ice can form on a camera shutter, causing it to freeze. Similarly ice on the lens diffuses the image.

Clothes

Clothing is most important in very cold conditions. Balaclava helmets and anoraks or hooded jackets are essential. Any wind will then be reduced and not be so cold to the head. Thick bodytight underwear helps general warmth and, when sitting in a hide a sleeping bag with a hot water bottle is very comforting. Knees are vulnerable to cold when sitting, so protect them with knee- or leg-warmers, and wear thick socks and mittens.

Snow

Snow produces very bright light which can be painful to the eyes. Protect them by wearing goggles with dark glass to reduce the glare. The light reading on your camera will be high especially when the sun is out. It will be difficult to trust your meter when these readings seem too high to be correct. Extra light may well be reflected onto your subject and into the lens. This is all right for the subject but not for the lens as it causes flare. A good lens hood is essential though a polarizing screen which comes in rotating mounts and can cut out flare from any highly reflective scene can eliminate the strong light by being carefully rotated to the correct position. With a pola screen it is possible to eliminate much of the reflection of skylight on the surface of water. In the process however it absorbs two stops of light. This is not a disadvantage in the snow because of the abnormally large amount of light present.

Wet conditions

Perhaps rain and damp cause most irritation to the photographer. Usually in such conditions there is too little light for any photography to be attempted, although there are exceptions. Showers with bright intervals often give the best light there is, and can produce attractive results using electronic flash.

A polythene bag wrapped round the camera protects it from the rain, and sometimes the camera can be operated from inside the bag. Always have a UV/haze filter over the end of all your lenses. This does not affect the colour or the speed of the lens but does cut out haze and shields the lens from physical damage and rain, though the latter produces a diffused and very soft image. A chamois leather wiped over the filter dries and cleans it enough to obtain good photographs intermittently, except in very heavy rain. A lens hood designed to prevent light falling onto the lens and causing flare, also serves to stop drizzle.

Bad weather does not mean that you have nothing to photograph. Some birds are not at all bothered by it; waterbirds live on water in any case, and others use rain as a means of washing or having a drink. A bird on its nest protects the young from a soaking by sitting on top of them. The beads of water on their backs make an attractive sight. Flashlight highlights this effect and is generally necessary to get the required depth of field.

Rain falling directly onto a flash head soon causes its malfunction as dampness interferes with the electrical circuits. Polythene bags completely surrounding the flash heads are the most satisfactory way of keeping out the rain. If the polythene is clear it will not interfere with the performance of the light output, though care must be taken to ensure that the automatic sensor is not covered up. Also ensure that the bag is covered up and does not flap as the noise can soon upset birds. If the battery is separate from the flash heads it can be protected in the same way.

If you are not properly prepared it can be most unpleasant working in a hide in the rain. Using the portable design with four corner poles supporting the canvas, heavy or prolonged rain produces a puddle on the roof to drip right into the centre of the hide either onto your camera or your head. Soon everything inside gets very damp. There are two ways of preventing this; one is to use a pole (like bamboo) and push it into the centre of the roof. You can sit at the side of it without too much inconvenience. The other is to use sticks in the roof to create diagonals from the four corners which again should prevent a large puddle gathering in the centre, though small ones may form at the edges. Once the rain is falling down the sides of the hide you can continue photography provided the camera lens is covered to stop water dripping down from the lens opening in the canvas. The entire camera can be enclosed in a large clear polythene bag by cutting a hole at one end for the lens hood and attaching it to the bag with tape. The rest of the camera can then be covered and operated through the bag or from the other end. This enables you to try for some dramatic shots in the rain. The biggest disadvantages are the noise the bag makes, and the difficulty of altering focus quickly from outside it.

Very heavy rain followed by hot sunshine always causes a problem with condensation on the lens and viewfinder. Again, a chamois leather or lens tissue are the answer when they mist over. If the front lens has a filter over it there should be no problem in wiping it clean and dry. Pulling it slowly into the hide and out again can usually be done without too much disturbance to the bird, though it is better to wait until the bird has just left the area and will not notice your movement.

If you intend doing a lot of hard weather photography it is advisable to build a more permanent hide. In cold wet conditions a wooden hide made from plywood is less draughty and warmer and more waterproof than one in canvas. Also there is nothing to flap in the wind, and it can be camouflaged easily with paint as well as having plants, small rocks, branches etc. put on the roof to add to its disguise. Have a small torch with you as a solid hide is very dark inside and you will want to read the settings on the camera. If you cannot read the settings without moving the camera, use a mirror.

Wind

The stability of both the camera and the hide can be affected badly by wind. Birds keep their distance from a flapping hide; it makes them suspicious and frightened. The camera, especially with a lengthy telephoto lens fitted, can be caught by the wind and the longer the lens the more this will be apparent. Therefore have your camera on a firm tripod to prevent this vibration. If you are outside with neither a hide nor a tripod, rest yourself and your camera against something stable. A screen which can be made quite easily from transparent plastic, helps to protect you in gusty conditions.

Summer

Winter leads to spring which for the bird photographer is the most exciting time of the year. The activity of courtship with birds wearing their finest plumage, and the beginnings of nest making and egg laying is a time full of potential. It is natural to want to spend more time out-of-doors with your camera when the weather is warmer, and this is, of course, when most birds are nesting. Thus the summer may seem a good time of year to begin photographing birds, but in fact taking pictures at the nest is a difficult aspect to start off with. Some species are nervous and when disturbed often desert a nest. Hopefully, all photographers feel that no photograph can justify this, and will not subject birds to stress of this kind. So start in your summer garden by providing nesting sites and material, both of which will give you excellent chances of photography.

Heat

Different countries of the world have a variety of habitats and climates. Working conditions therefore, vary considerably between hot and wet, cold and dry. In more temperate zones one experiences a combination of these with neither heat nor cold being a great problem. Photographic equipment is usually fairly robust and capable of standing up to a range of conditions. In any situation there are always precautions you can take to protect both yourself and your equipment. Take plenty of film with you wherever you go especially in remote areas, as it may well be that none will be available locally or even near your location.

Sunlight can produce dramatic effects on a proposed subject, but it also causes considerable problems both to the camera and the operator as soon as you attempt photography in and around the tropics. If staying in a hot region for only a few days you will probably not incur too many problems, so most of the points mentioned below will be irrelevant. But for those who live in a hot climate or who plan to visit one for some time, there are several factors to consider. Clear objectives are important even when working with a common species; it is always better to try for a definite end result. In warmer countries bird life is more abundant and colourful. The first temptation is to go after too many different subjects as a vast range of opportunities present themselves. This is never very satisfactory as you may end up with few pictures that please you. Unless you have a plan in mind for the fieldwork you hope to achieve heat may well overcome you before you really start serious work. If you live in a hot region you will be accustomed to the climate and know more about the birds than if you are a visitor. With this fundamental conditioning to the climate you will be aware of your own capabilities and therefore able to make clear decisions.

Heat produces three main problems to photographic equipment; one obviously is the high temperature, and the others are humidity in the wet areas of the tropics, and dust and sand in the drier areas.

Humidity

The water present in a hot damp atmosphere encourages the growth of mould on equipment and film, which can cause serious damage. If a lens is left unused for a few weeks a mould growth can soon start on the glass and become bad enough to break up the image when it is being used. The only way to remove it might be to have the lens repolished which is costly. Prevention is always better then cure, regular cleaning and inspection should become a matter of course with all equipment. The best way is to store everything in an airtight container with a moisture absorbing compound inside. Silica-gel is probably the most widely used, is relatively cheap and can be used for ever. Baking it in an oven reactivates it and ensures that it is completely dry and should last for many months. It is possible to obtain some that changes colour when it becomes fully saturated. Metal cases holding equipment with silica-gel inside are very useful. A light reflective surface ensures that sunlight is bounced off rather than absorbed. These cases are strong enough to be sat on, and ideally should be watertight. If they are not any anhydrous compound will soon become saturated from humidity leaking into the case.

Tins sealed with tape make good airtight containers, though they can be awkward shapes for carrying around. One of the most useful accessories for all types of conditions is the polythene bag. It is light and easily sealed and has the beauty of showing what is inside without the seal being undone. Each piece of equipment can then have its own bag with silica-gel inside it.

If you live in the tropics it is possible to make a box or container at home for your equipment that can be kept at a higher temperature than the surroundings by means of additional heating like a light bulb. The increased temperature will eliminate most of the humidity. It may well be impractical to leave continuous power on and should not be attempted above 115°F as this will affect the mechanics of a camera. Storage by either of these methods means removing the film from your camera as over drying the emulsion can spoil it, and overheating can affect the colour balance and cause it to become sticky and even melt. At the end of the day you may still have a few exposures left. In more temperate climates you can rewind the film to the beginning and reload it another time by counting the recorded number of exposures. But with such a film in hot conditions, because the emulsion is softer, there is a much greater risk of scratching from anything sticking to it by winding it in and out of the cassette. The best policy is to waste the unused end of the film to ensure the safety of the exposures already made.

The film stock itself is best kept in the manufacturers' sealed containers until just before it is needed. Long term storage should be in a refrigerator but a few weeks at 100°F should be all right provided it is kept in its original packing. In a hot atmosphere constantly taking film in and out of a fridge is more likely to upset the colour balance than letting it remain at a constant temperature whether it is warm or cold.

Dry heat

In desert regions there is very little moisture present but, although this means no humidity problems, it introduces dust particles and very high temperatures. As sand and fine particles can seemingly penetrate anywhere causing a lot of trouble with photographic equipment, cameras and lenses need covering at all times. Lenses can have UV filters on them, not only to give a better colour saturation, but also to protect the front element of the lens. Polythene bags again come in useful and, being light, can be carried about all the time. Linen and leather bags are very good too as equipment can be taken from them without too much noise. A combination of two or three bags provides efficient protection from dust and sand. Regular cleaning every day is the best way to prevent equipment from becoming spoilt from dust. Lenses can be cleaned inside and out with a blower brush and polythene bags can be changed regularly. A set time every day is the best discipline.

Changing film is difficult if there is wind about as sand in the back of the camera soon causes failures. Have a changing bag with you as part of your standard gear in case a film gets jammed when you are far from a darkroom. Also, in very dry conditions, they are wonderful for changing a film as you can operate with the camera and film safely out of the wind, thereby preventing any dust reaching the inside. In very hot conditions your hands may sweat working in the close confines of a bag. All you can do is to be as careful as you can not to touch the film. Buy as large a bag as is practical to carry around. If you have a supply of water, cooling your hands first helps, and wherever possible try and work in the shade.

Exposed film

Once film is exposed it should be processed as soon as possible to get the best results. Many of you may have had a film in your camera for some time before it is finished. This should not matter too much provided the camera is kept in sensible places when not being used. Never for instance leave it out in direct sunlight as it can quickly become too hot to handle.

It is always desirable to keep film as cool as possible before or after exposure. If you have to keep it once it is exposed, put it back into its sealed container and make sure it is somewhere not affected by too much heat. Keeping colour film too long will have the effect of altering the colour balance which, for birds, is often a serious disadvantage as it changes the appearance of the plumage. Black and white film has much greater latitude. Moisture can be very damaging and once on the exposed emulsion causes marks that cannot be removed. Always pack film on a dry day and keep it in sealed containers.

Try to change a film in the shade so that no direct sunlight falls onto it. Keep it well away from unexposed film as, particularly with 35 mm, it is easy to inadvertently put an exposed film back into the camera. To make sure this never happens always wind the film right back into the cassette so that you cannot even see the end of it. This ensures both that you do not use it again, and also that the processors have to break the cassette open to get at the film. If you send films to process with the leader still out the temptation is just to pull the film out without opening the cassette. That introduces the risk of a tramline scratch down the whole length of the film if any grit has become stuck in the felt opening. Look at the cassette each time you put a film in the camera to check that you cannot see anything likely to cause such damage. Many people load their own film from long lengths into reloadable cassettes. Tramline damage is always a risk so look out for it. If you are spending several days in the heat a way to keep film cool is to bury it in the ground wrapped in plastic bags in sealed tins.

Travelling with equipment

Travelling with film also puts it at risk from X-ray damage. A special foil covering surrounding all the film is the best arrangement. Bags for this purpose can be bought. They will withstand all but the strongest X-ray checking machines. But, X-rays having a cumulative effect, they cannot be passed through more than a few times before the film is damaged. I carry all exposed film with me as hand luggage to be sure it is safe and not left behind.

Camera and lenses are delicate so your method of transportation is important. Strong cases with firm support inside for each piece of equipment, is ideal. Equipment carried in metal cases with foam rubber is fairly safe from knocks which could cause mechanical trouble or misalignment of a lens. Wooden cases are strong but very heavy to carry around. In hot climates it is important to keep the equipment as cool as possible, so cases in a light metallic colour or painted white prevent it from absorbing too much heat. I prefer metal cases; they are strong and fairly light and many times I end up using one as a seat.

It is not always convenient to carry the case with all the extras over a large field area, so for a single day's photography wrap each piece of equipment you need separately and carry them in a rucksack. Partitions inside are useful; each item has its own place and you can tell at a glance if anything is missing.

Birds in hot climates

Although many exciting species can be found in hot climates they are not necessarily easy to approach, and their nests are hard to find.

Birds do not all breed in the same season so some knowledge of particular species is necessary to prevent fruitless searching. Introducing hides needs as much caution as in cool climates. Birds nesting in places subjected to direct sun have only themselves to protect the eggs or young from the heat. Any disturbance of more than 5 minutes can be enough for the sun to kill the eggs so cover them during any stage of hide-building to prevent this. Work must be carried out quickly and safely and if immediate acceptance is not apparent the hide must be removed again.

Not only does direct sun produce heat problems, it also makes very hard shadows which often give more contrast than colour materials can cope with. Black and white in these cases is easier to control.

Contrast is best controlled by use of fill in flash. Adjustment of the power and position of the flash will depend on how strong the highlight reading is for the subject. As the day progresses the flash head will need to be moved to correspond with the sun. At midday in the tropics the sun is directly overhead causing a dense shadow underneath the bird. Being the hottest part of the day it can become unbearable in a hide so the best plan is to stop photography until the sun has moved to an angle where it produces more modelling in the subject and becomes a little cooler.

Working in more wooded surroundings there will be strong dappled light falling through the leaves which causes a mixture of strong highlights and heavy shadow so that fill in flash must be used to provide even lighting. Two flash heads may well be necessary in some of the more dense areas, and care must be taken to choose a suitable background to light or one that is naturally lit and can be well balanced with flash.

If attempting to photograph a well hidden nest take great care not to open up the surrounding foliage. Predation is high at the best of times and thoughtless actions can quickly result in failure. In some countries the local inhabitants are as likely to predate your nest as animals or other birds, so concealment of a hide is as important here as anywhere. Heat in a hide can make working very difficult. Ventilation holes at the top and sides are helpful, especially if there is any breeze. In still air the heat can become intense and cause you to sweat profusely; a cold drink from a thermos gives relief. In these conditions birds are likely to be quite inactive, so the best time to photograph them is at the end of the day. The morning is often a good time as well; being cooler the birds are more lively and it is more comfortable for working. The nearer you are to the tropics the shorter the twilight is. The sun rises and goes down more quickly than in distant latitudes away from the equator. The hotter it becomes the more welcome a shaded area such as a hide, is going to be to insects, snakes and other creatures. This obviously presents difficulties, the most annoying of which will be the insects and flies. Use anti-insect spray inside the hide to stop insects buzzing around, though newcomers will find their way in sooner or later. A hat with a net or gauze hanging on the front will at least prevent flies from landing on your face.

Hot climates make very good places for lures. Any food is quickly eaten by insects and other animals so any available food that you have can be put out regularly to attract a number of birds. Water is an obvious pull especially in areas where it is scarce. A dripping supply from a holed bucket in a tree onto the ground will soon attract attention. A pool will be regularly visited giving ample chance at whatever comes along. The thrill of the unexpected is usually well rewarded in this way.

Environment

The sea environment contains many species of birds that feed and breed in and near it. Seabird colonies are frequently found on islands seldom visited by humans and as a result some are quite tame. Sometimes it is possible to take good photographs without a hide. However, the birds themselves are always going to be aware of you and any concentrated study of colonial birds, or of individuals, is best done from the concealment of an accepted hide, where the birds will not be aware of your presence.

Sea, seashore and estuary

Many birds spend all their non-breeding time at sea miles away from land. To us it always seems a hostile environment, but the birds are well adapted to it. Photographing in winter is extremely difficult. The advent of the breeding season finds birds with distinct plumages, different from and sometimes, more colourful, than their winter feathers. Photographs showing the difference would be of interest. The only chance to photograph them is from a boat at sea. Some birds apparently disappear during the winter months—no one knows exactly where they go. The glimpse from a passing boat may be all that you get. The sea's motion and the vibration of the boat make it almost impossible to keep the subject in the viewfinder. Using a 400 mm or 35 mm lens you can get acceptable results showing birds sitting on or flying over the water. It is best to use a fast film so that you can use as fast a shutter speed as possible to get a sharp image. Gulls often follow boats closely, and can be successfully photographed with a shorter focal length lens (135 mm). Boats attract migrants who perch on the rigging at night, remaining until dawn. This gives more opportunities for unusual pictures.

The seashore and estuaries are very fertile regions. They support a wealth of life, all of which is potential food for different kinds of birds. Wading birds make the most of this food though sea birds and geese are glad of it during migration, and in winter many other species also feed by the sea. Both the food supply and birds are regulated by tidal action and your work might have to be also. 'Wait-and-see' hides are probably the most successful for photographing birds being forced up a beach by the tide. Place your hide near to popular feeding grounds and you are sure to get some good shots. On open sites as many of these tend to be, you *must* have a hide that does not flap. One of conventional height is likely to be too high for some birds used to feeding amidst large horizons. Although uncomfortable, a hide at half height will probably give the birds more confidence. Kneeling in waders on mud flats inside the hide should give you enough room to operate the camera on a tripod. In winter the mud can be very cold to the knees and you will be in trouble if the tide comes in too far, so site your hide carefully. If it is well placed a 135 mm lens will be sufficient to give you detailed shots of individuals, but in practice a 400 mm may well provide more opportunities if no birds come as close as you had hoped.

Lakes, ponds and marshes

Many birds breed on or near water. In marshy areas small pylon structures are necessary to achieve a sound base and correct walking height for the camera. Fine netting to protect your face and an insecticide inside the hide help protect you against insects, especially mosquitoes, that are inevitable in these environs and are maddening both for their whine and their bites.

Birds nesting in or near water must be approached just as cautiously as land birds. A firm base for your tripod is necessary, and this often means making a platform at the edge of the lake on which to build the rest of a hide by degrees. Have the camera at a fairly low angle so that you can work close to water level for birds that build floating nests. The level usually remains constant with fresh water lakes and ponds.

A lake's depth dictates the type of plant life growing there, and

1 Photographing from a boat. Thick netting or sacking can be used to cover you.   **2** Using thick bundles of reeds as an effective floating hide, either for a nest over several days or for waterfowl in a 'wait and see' situation.

also the birds attracted to it. Diving ducks inhabit deep lakes, while dabbling ducks and waders are found on shallow water.

Hides on water

Many lakes contain considerable amounts of aquatic plant life which attracts geese and ducks alike. Large concentrations of these build up at the end of the breeding season and during winter. This makes a pleasing sight for the photographer, but also, unfortunately, for the hunter. Shooting is so popular that only certain areas of wetland are protected from it. The scale of hunting has become such, that ducks and geese particularly, have become very wild and unapproachable, and consequently hard to photograph. It is possibly easier while they are feeding. Use a boat adapted as a hide. You can obtain some results by lying, camouflaged, in a flat punt-like vessel, drifting and paddling very slowly. By making use of available cover you may approach to within 100 ft or so. A more upright design can have bunches of reeds or similar vegetation all round it. By anchoring in one spot or manoeuvring as before, you can get within range. The disadvantage of any kind of boat is that it is constantly moving, and it is therefore very difficult to maintain a steady picture even on a tripod. Concealment in reeds can well produce good opportunities for taking flying birds overhead. Many geese have particular flight lines and directions in which they fly at certain times of the day and season. A well placed hide on a hillside can produce flying as well as grazing geese as they have temporary favourite fields in which to eat, often near lakes where they spend the night.

Temperate grasslands

This habitat occupies large areas of land called 'the prairies' in North America, the 'steppe lands' in Eurasia, the 'veld' in South Africa, and the 'pampas' in South America. They are predominantly open grass with a small amount of annual rainfall. Numerically speaking there are fewer birds here than in the forests, though due to the lack of cover (except for grass) they are often well camouflaged and difficult to see. Some of them have characteristic nests which makes the field work a little easier if you are searching for a particular species.

Grasslands in summer are hot and working from a hide has many of the problems discussed earlier. Introduction in open country necessitates several days. In some cases a flat hide in which you can lie in may be a quicker way to gain a bird's confidence though because of the welcome shade it may provide, snakes and other creatures move in, which can mean a certain amount of inconvenience.

Game birds are found in this habitat and can be baited with corn either loose or on the cob, or with many other different seeds. Good shrub cover near the feeding area increases the chance of birds staying by the bait.

Stretches of water in the grassland regions are a tremendous attraction and many species breed here in large numbers during spring and summer.

Domestic ranching of livestock has been happening for some time, so related mammal-bird photographs are to be found here as elsewhere. Beware of their animosity.

Forests

The strong growth of trees and the often thick cover beneath them, provide a wide selection of habitats for birds. The ground, low shrubs, bushes, trees large and small, hollow trees and holes in roots and rocks, all provide excellent nesting sites. The range is extensive, especially in a mature forest and a corresponding variety of birds is to be found.

With more warmth and rainfall, the resulting forests and their high species diversity, will hold the greatest number of different bird species. Photographic problems might be numerous. Dense vegetation means that flash will often be necessary, and warm forests are humid which upsets electrics. Many subjects will be up in the trees which entails a lot of difficult work building hides in the branches or erecting structures which usually have to be made of wood from the immediately available materials.

Concentrate on the easier subjects to locate, and be selective in finding an attractive site. Extra hours of fieldwork to chose the 'right' place are always worth it. It is pointless to handicap yourself unnecessarily by working in surroundings which are never going to look good. Many forests contain fascinating plant life so hunt about for example, for an attractive fern to use in your photograph. Woodland species can be shy even though available cover may make introduction of a hide comparatively easy. However the reverse is often true with a few birds appearing tamer than you would expect. Birds, like humans, vary in personality and it is not uncommon to find one bird of one species to be approachable and another of the same species to be quite the opposite.

Mountains

Mountains, hills and cliffs are challenging places for bird photography. In addition to the photographic problems, there are others related to the terrain to be walked over and the height at which you will work. Stamina with physical exertion is usually a requisite for success here, together with a head for heights and competence at negotiating steep rocky paths.

The scenery alone is often sufficient to warrant the use of a camera. Visually stimulating countryside, whether on a mountain or not, has the photographer always on the lookout for ways of incorporating it into his photographs. The bird photographer will wish to do the same. Many birds of prey live and breed in this kind of habitat, their nests usually being in inaccessible places which mean a considerable effort to get a photograph. Baiting in the winter on hillsides and mountains can be most productive if it is possible to make regular visits to put out food. By using carrion bait in a conspicuous position you might find it possible to take a bird on a branch or rock with a commanding view of the background. A shot like this can say a lot more about the bird than a more conventional nest photograph. Birds of prey are extremely wary and suspicious. Because of their incredibly keen eyesight careful steps must be taken near any nest as they can easily desert their eggs. Caution always pays off, so wait until eggs hatch before you approach. Many species are protected so find out about all the restrictions on disturbance both locally and internationally. Building a hide on a cliff-face is not easy. Try to get someone who has built one before to come along and help you build it. Again this should be spread over several days though you must work fast and not for more than 40 minutes in a day in order not to keep an anxious parent away for longer than absolutely necessary. Never build a section or make a move late in the day, whether with a bird of prey or any other bird. Distress causing the bird not to return as it gets dark may well result in it not returning at all once darkness has fallen. This would be disastrous for small young. It is therefore best to make any moves or changes to the hide earlier in the day so that you have plenty of time to observe whether or not the bird is accepting your actions. At altitude make sure again that all the canvas is really tight; use plenty of rocks to prevent any possibility of flapping.

Introducing a hide onto a steep hillside can be a problem as it can easily fall over. Erect the front at half height and the back at normal height; if you have expandable poles they will come into their own here.

Working at altitude in the mornings and evenings, the sun shines from a very low angle which can be used to advantage to show the underside of flying birds' wings. Otherwise this would be impossible. Birds of prey are great soaring creatures that glide on warm updraughts of air. Flight shots are always a possibility as thermals rising and general wind both produce currents of air. Vultures and similar species will only be seen in the air when the temperature is warm enough to create sufficient thermals which may be a few hours after sunrise. Frequently it entails a tiring climb to a vantage point so you are automatically limited to the amount of equipment you can carry. A shoulder pod and a 400 mm can provide you with a good chance on hills. It is not always practical to take a tripod but you can find support by leaning against a tree or lying down on rocks which can support the camera lens. A monopod is light and easy to use as it can double as a walking stick particularly if it has a Y-fork at the top for holding the lens. After such a strenuous climb you will be unable to hold the camera steady because of vibration from your increased heart rate so you will need support of some kind.

Appendix

Bird photography and the law

In the United Kingdom all wild birds' nests and young are protected by law. In other countries of the world protection is not necessarily so complete. Different laws apply in different regions so no hard and fast rules can be applied everywhere.

The rarer birds are afforded the maximum protection and in Britain it is necessary to obtain a licence to photograph or disturb any of the species in Schedule 1 of the *Protection of Birds Acts 1954–1976*. This licence is obtainable by writing to the Nature Conservancy Council (N.C.C.), 19 Belgrade Square, London SW1X 8PY. This often means that for some species which occur abroad, it may well be easier to go there to photograph them where they are probably more abundant.

Licences are unlikely to be granted for rarer birds in places where they are scarce. Also it is necessary to be able to show you are photographically competent from submission of examples of your work from commoner species. A successful application for a licence does *not* give you permission to trespass on private land. Landowners permission is always required as well.

Throughout the world as conservation becomes a stronger voice there are many sanctuaries set up and in the process of being established where entry is totally prohibited, affording complete protection to all creatures within its boundaries. For the very rare birds this is straightforward commonsense. With some such places entry is on a restricted basis and it may well be that photography can be attempted from permanent observation hides. Local enquiries will soon establish the situation.

Schedule 1 Species

Avocet
Bee-eater (all species)
Bittern (all species)
Bluethroat
Brambling
Bunting, Snow
Bustard
Buzzard, Honey
Chough
Corncrake, Landrail
Crake, Spotted
Crossbill, Common
Curlew, Stone
Diver (all species)
Dotterel
Eagle (all species)
Fieldfare
Firecrest
Garganey
Godwit, Black-tailed
Goldeneye
Goshawk
Grebe, Black-necked
Greve, Slavonian
Greenshank
Harrier (all species)
Hobby
Hoopoe
Kingfisher
Kite
Duck, Long-tailed
Merlin
Oriole, Golden
Osprey
Owl, Barn (England and Wales only)
Owl, Snowy (Scotland only)

Peregrine
Phalarope, Red-necked
Plover, Kentish
Plover, Little ringed
Quail, Common
Quail, European
Redstart, Black
Redwing
Roller
Ruff
Reeve
Sandpiper, Wood
Scaup
Scoter, Common
Serin
Shrike, Red-backed (England and Wales only)
Sparrowhawk (England and Wales only)
Spoonbill
Stilt, Black-winged
Stint, Temminck's
Swan, Bewick's
Swan, Whooper
Tern, Black
Tern, Little
Tern, Roseate
Tit, Bearded
Tit, Crested
Velvet scoter
Warbler, Dartford
Warbler, Marsh
Warbler, Savi's
Whimbrel
Woodlark
Wren, St Kilda
Wryneck

The Royal Society for the Protection of Birds, The Lodge, Sandy, Bedfordshire SG19 2DL, England, have a leaflet *Wild Birds and the Law* (price approximately 10p) which provides more detailed information on all matters of the law and birds in the UK.

Index